THE CALEDONIAN DUNALASTAIRS

David & Charles Locomotive Monographs

General Editor:
O. S. NOCK, B.Sc., C.Eng., M.I.C.E., F.I.Mech.E., M.I.Loco.E.

Published titles

The Midland Compounds, by O. S. Nock

The Stirling Singles of the Great Northern Railway, by Kenneth H. Leech and Maurice Boddy

The LNWR Precursor Family, by O. S. Nock

The GWR Stars, Castles & Kings, Part 1, by O. S. Nock

The Caledonian Dunalastairs, by O. S. Nock

In preparation

The GWR Stars, Castles & Kings, Part 2, by O. S. Nock

The Gresley Pacifics, by O. S. Nock

One of the superheated 'Dunalastair IV' class engines No 120

DAVID & CHARLES LOCOMOTIVE MONOGRAPHS

THE CALEDONIAN DUNALASTAIRS

AND ASSOCIATED CLASSES

O. S. NOCK, B.Sc., C.Eng., M.I.C.E., F.I.Mech.E., M.I.Loco.E.

DAVID & CHARLES   :   NEWTON ABBOT   :   DEVON

7153 4251 7

First published in 1968 by
David & Charles (Holdings) Ltd
Newton Abbot Devon

Printed in Great Britain by
W J Holman Ltd Dawlish Devon

CONTENTS

PREFACE

THE Caledonian 'Dunalastairs' rank as one of the most remarkable locomotive families in history. The purists will say at once that some of the engines described in this book were not strictly 'Dunalastairs'; but the Drummonds and the Lambies, which form the prelude, and the Pickersgills which formed a long-lived epilogue to the story, are all so much interwoven with the saga of locomotive designing and building at St Rollox as to be indivisible from the central massif of the 'Dunalastairs' proper: the types for which J. F. McIntosh was directly responsible. There are some who would say that the Pickersgills make an anti-climax to the story. As first-class express passenger engines one must admit that this is largely so. By their very longevity, however, the Pickersgills earned a special place in the memories and affec-tions of railway enthusiasts, and by their massive reliability they came to fill a very useful niche in the motive power strategy of the Scottish Region of British Railways.

Many friends have contributed to the making of this book. I am first of all indebted to British Rail-ways Scottish Region for making available to me copies of many of the general arrangement and detail drawings of the engines concerned, and for supplying photographs. Messrs Campbell Cornwell, Alan G. Dunbar, Alastair McPhail, and A. J. S. Paterson have between them provided me with a mass of factual data on which to work, while Messrs A. G. Ellis and T. V. R. Barbour have made available to me magnificent collections of photo-graphs, the latter mailed to me from Rhodesia. Through the kindness of Mr A. E. Robson, Chief

Dunalastair Post Office : centre of a very scattered district in Perthshire

9

Engineer Rolling Stock, British Railways Board, I have been able to use reports of the dynamometer car trials of engine No 124 between Carlisle and Leeds in December 1924, and in 1934 I had the privilege of riding on Pickersgill 4—4—0s in express service between Glasgow and Aberdeen.

Another source of fascinating contemporary information has been the diaries of the late Lord Monkswell, and some quotations from them are included by courtesy of Lady Monkswell. I have also been able to quote extensively from details of engine performance published in *The Engineer*, *Engineering* and *The Railway Magazine*, by courtesy of the present editors of those journals. I am also much indebted to Mr B. W. Pendred, editor-in-chief of *The Engineer*, and Mr F. B. Roberts, editor of *Engineering*, for permission to reproduce certain drawings and diagrams previously published in those journals.

Lastly, as always, I am very grateful for the help of Olivia, my wife, who joined me in a motor-car expedition in Scotland to try and find Dunalastair itself. It is marked on the map, but the cottages proved so scattered that when we eventually reached the 'centre' of the clachan, the post office, there was not another house or building or any kind within sight!

O. S. NOCK

Silver Cedars
High Bannerdown
Batheaston, Bath
September 1967

CHAPTER 1

THE DRUMMOND PRELUDE: 1882-1895

ON 15 April 1890 there was a meeting of the Board of Directors of the Caledonian Railway, and one item on the agenda was to receive a letter of resignation from Dugald Drummond, their locomotive superintendent. Although this resignation was received with great regret it had been anticipated to the extent that applications to fill the vacancy were considered at that same meeting, and Hugh Smellie of the Glasgow & South Western Railway was chosen as Drummond's successor. There is no doubt, however, that when the board received news of the impending resignation of Dugald Drummond they were taken by surprise. He was then just fifty years of age, and earning one of the highest salaries paid to any British locomotive engineer at that time. His work on the Caledonian, as designer, manufacturer and administrator had been a long succession of successes, and until he received the ill-fated offer of a fabulous position in Australia his career seemed assured on every count.

With all respect to the men who immediately followed him, his going left a profound gap at St Rollox. Smellie died within a year of being appointed, and John Lambie who followed him was fifty-eight years of age at the time of his appointment. For a period of four years he continued the Drummond traditions, building new locomotives that differed no more than superficially from their predecessors, but which nevertheless achieved renown from their spectacular work in the Race to the North in 1895. Lambie died early in 1895, and in February of that year John Farquharson McIntosh was appointed to succeed him. Although the new chief was like Drummond in the possession of an extremely strong personality, the likeness ended there; for although McIntosh was already a great railwayman he was no theorist, no engine-designer, but instead a very practical running man, and a strong administrator. His position was similar to that of George Whale on the London & North Western Railway. McIntosh had a clear conception of the kind of engine needed to work the traffic, and he gave the drawing office no more than a broad outline of his wishes. But before coming to the very fine locomotives produced under his direction it is necessary to take much more than a passing glance at the 4—4—0s of the 1882-95 period, for in most respects they formed the basis of the great success achieved by the locomotive department of the Caledonian Railway during the McIntosh regime.

The story commences in 1884, when Neilson & Co delivered the first examples of the celebrated '66' class of Drummond 4—4—0s. The basic dimensions were commonplace enough: cylinders 18 in diameter by 26 in stroke; coupled wheels 6 ft 6 in diameter, and boiler pressure 150 psi. They were slender-looking, graceful engines, distinguished outwardly by having the Ramsbottom safety valves on the top of the dome. Within that slender exterior Drummond incorporated some of the most advanced thinking of the day in locomotive engineering. In some ways he anticipated the work of Churchward on the Great Western, some twenty years later, for he gave the closest attention to the utilisation of steam in the cylinders, and was thus able to supply all the needs of a relatively powerful 'engine' from quite a small boiler. Although the original engines of 1884 had boilers carrying 150 psi, the later engines of the class built in 1889 and 1891 had steel boilers designed to take a pressure of 200 psi.

Drummond aimed to secure fully expansive working, from a wide-open regulator and short cut-offs, thereby obviating any need to resort to compounding. But the use of high boiler pressure alone was not enough to ensure the economical use of steam in the cylinders, and Drummond gave particular attention to the design of the ports and

Dugald Drummond : from a pencil portrait in 'The Bailie', June 1884

were increased so that the belt from the lower and top valves extended along the whole length of the cylinder thus forming an exhaust steam jacketed cylinder. The blast pipe, which was of the Vortex-type, had likewise a large exhaust capacity with a nozzle equal to a 5 in opening.'

It is important to appreciate, however, that the fore-end layout to which Drummond was referring, and which gave such remarkable results in the 1889 trials to be mentioned later, was not standard throughout the class. The design used on the first sixteen engines, Nos 60-75, built in 1884-5, followed that used on the North British '476' class of 1876, which in turn was derived from Stroudley's practice. These engines also had the divided steam ports, while steam leaving the lower portion of the exhaust port passed round the cylinder in a cast passage before joining the steam from the upper portion at the base of the blastpipe. In the engines built in 1880, which were used in the trials, the steam ports instead of being towards the centre of the valve face were moved to the ends, giving a very short and direct passage. Furthermore, separate exhaust ports were provided at each end of the valve face, as Drummond described in his paper, and the total port area for exhaust was doubled.

The result was a remarkably free-running engine which was economical in fuel consumption and which produced a very high output of power in relation to the cylinder dimensions and boiler pressure. Some details of trials made in 1889, between Edinburgh and Carlisle, give particulars of performance from four different engines of the 6 ft 6 in express passenger class. At that time Drummond was experimenting with higher boiler pressures. While the standard pressure then in use was 150 psi, one engine of those selected for test was using 175 psi and two others no less than 200

slide valves. In a paper published in the Proceedings of the Institution of Civil Engineers 1896-7, the arrangement was described thus: 'The design of the cylinders is a departure from the normal arrangement with a central valve-face. The steam ports were moved to the cylinder-ends and the slide valve was divided, each having its own exhaust port. In this way the port-clearance was reduced to a minimum, and a reduction in back pressure was effected. The weight of the valve, however, was increased by 70 per cent. The exhaust passages

Engine No 79 'Carbrook', a Drummond 4—4—0 at one time carrying a boiler pressure of 200 lb per sq in

Engine No 124 'Eglinton', at one time fitted with the Bryce-Douglas valve gear

psi. Engine No 78, which six years later did some wonderful work in the 1895 Race to the North, did good work; but in the 1889 trials she was completely outclassed by No 79, carrying a boiler pressure of 200 psi. The following is a selection of performances by engine No 79:

Speed mph	Regulator opening	Cut-off per cent	Indicated horsepower
51	Full	27	940
65½	Full	19	553
57½	Full	21	766
65	Full	22	770
37	Full	33	856
33¼	Full	33	806

Despite the fact that the 200 lb engines did considerably the fastest work, with similarly loaded trains, their coal consumption was much the least of the four.

It is remarkable to find a locomotive of this vintage, developing nearly 1,000 indicated horsepower, at 51 mph, as No 79 achieved, and this engine was at one time successfully worked in as short a cut-off as 13 per cent.

In the concluding paragraphs of his paper Drummond was clearly thinking of his then-colleague at Crewe, for he wrote:

'During part of the running of engine No 76, five expansions were made, the efficiency increasing to the highest point. As the whole question of engine-economy resolves itself into the number of times steam can be expanded, and as in this case five expansions were within the economical limit in a single cylinder, compounding within this limit appears to be unnecessary. If, however, the thermal and dynamical conditions of the non-compound are superior to those of the compound engine, how is it that those who favour the latter system have attained superior results? The reply must be that the two systems have not been compared on a fair basis. In the first place, the boiler pressure of the compound locomotive has been usually higher. In the second place, the driver of the compound engine is obliged to keep up the boiler pressure, as there must be considerably less range of mean cylinder-pressure than in the non-compound engines which can expand steam as low as one-and-a-quarter times, and all starting from stations is so done—whereas the compound locomotive cannot expand less than two-and-a-half times. This reduction of range in the power of the latter engine is undoubtedly the cause of reduced coal consumption over what is due

Engine No	Boiler pressure psi	Average speed mph				Coal consumption round trip lb/mile
		Edinburgh-Strawfrank	Strawfrank-Carlisle	Carlisle-Strawfrank	Strawfrank-Edinburgh	
76	200	49·2	51·0	51·0	53·9	45·9
77	175	50·6	52·3	46·2	56·6	44·4
78	150	49·2	52·6	43·7	53·9	53·2
79	200	52·2	53·9	49·6	59·7	42·3

*One of the Lambie 4—4—0s, No 17, and maker of the record run from Perth to
Aberdeen on the last night of the Race of 1895*

to higher boiler pressure. Other things being equal, coal consumption is the measure of the work done by an engine, and if the compound engine cannot run so fast in express traffic, or has to be assisted on up-gradients, the result should not be credited to increased efficiency. The Author is of the opinion that in a comparative trial of the simple and compound systems, the boiler pressure should be alike. The minimum number of expansions should be alike; and the low-pressure cylinder of the compound engine should be equal to the combined areas of the non-compound cylinders. On this common basis only should the trials be conducted, and no analysis offers greater advantages than the one adopted here. He suggests that such a test should be made with engines on the compound principle against non-compound engines say for a month's duration, in order that their respective merits may be tested in a way that will settle doubts existing on the question.'

At the same time he evidently did not consider that the results he had obtained with engines 76 and 79 were realisable in everyday running. He found difficulty in getting his drivers to work with short cut-offs, and in such circumstances much of the advantage of high boiler pressures was thrown away. Evidently, on the Caledonian in the 'eighties' of the last century, it was not considered possible to educate the enginemen, as Churchward so successfully did on the Great Western some twenty years later, and Drummond concluded:

'Viewing the question of steam pressures broadly, the Author has come to the conclusion that for the present, until drivers appreciate the value and take advantage of higher pressures for ordinary locomotive engines working main line traffic economically in all respects, the pressure should not be less than 150 lb. nor more than 170 lb. per sq. in. Pressures of 200 lb. per square inch can, he believes, only be economically used with engines working heavy suburban passenger-traffic, whereby speed can be got up quickly when leaving stations.'

*A Lambie 4—4—0 No 14 on the 10 am Edinburgh-Euston corridor dining-car train
posed at Princes St Station, Edinburgh*

Despite the remarkable technical results he had achieved Drummond evidently did not consider that the refinements of cylinder design, quite apart from the higher boiler pressures, were worth the candle, and in six more 4—4—0 express engines built in 1891 he reverted to the original fore-end layout of 1884, except that there was a slight variation in the valve setting. The original engines of 1884 had $4\frac{3}{16}$ in valve travel in full gear, a steam lap of 1 in, and a lead in full gear of $\frac{3}{16}$ in. The engines of 1889 and 1891 had the lead reduced to $\frac{1}{8}$ in. Any reduction of the lead tends to provide greater power, demonstrated by a 'fatter' indicator diagram, and on the Great Western Churchward's standard design of the Stephenson link motion included a *negative* amount of lead in full gear, so as to provide only the minimum needed for free running when the engine was fully linked up.

Nevertheless, although he had to some extent failed in one of his objectives, Drummond had carried out a great pioneer work on the Caledonian Railway, which Lambie followed up in his new 4—4—0 engines of 1894. In these latter the boiler pressure was increased to 160 psi, and they proved supremely fast runners. In the Race to the North in 1895, the Lambie engines set new standards of performance, by running at sustained speeds of 75 mph on level track. At that time maximum speeds of 75 mph, 80 and even 85 mph were frequent enough when running downhill, but such a speed of 75 mph on the level was something quite new, and it anticipated the running of the Great Western 'City' class 4—4—0s in the high-speed runs of 1903 and 1904. The official drawings of the front-end of the Lambie 4—4—0 show clearly the steam-jacketed cylinders, and Vortex blastpipe. It is also of particular interest to find that the drawing, in addition to John Lambie's signature bears the initials 'R.W.U.'—that is Robert Urie, who was then chief draughtsman at St Rollox, and who afterwards joined Dugald Drummond on the London & South Western Railway, and eventually succeeded him as chief mechanical engineer.

In 1895 all the elements of outstanding success were present at St Rollox. Dugald Drummond, a shrewd and far-sighted engine designer, had laid down the great principles for development: higher boiler pressures, and cylinders in which a minimum of power would be wasted, by throttling at admission and exhaust. He was backed up by a magnificent drawing office staff, under Robert Urie, and a running department that was prepared to 'lick the pants' off anyone. Both Lambie and McIntosh were 'running men', and McIntosh in particular had ample experience of the working of

John Lambie

the Drummond locomotives. He took office in the flood-tide of success. In 1895 the Caledonian and its locomotives had won imperishable fame. There was no 'delicate' situation to be nurtured, as when Churchward began to take the reins at Swindon, from Dean's failing hands; there was no debâcle, as had developed in Webb's last years at Crewe. McIntosh took over in an atmosphere of general

THE DOWN 'TOURIST' EXPRESS
Load : 138 tons tare, 145 tons full
Engine : Drummond 4—4—0 No 61

Dist miles			Actual m s	Av speeds mph
0·0	PERTH	. .	0 00	
4·2	Luncarty	.	6 10	
5·1	Strathord	. .	7 13	51·4
7·2	Stanley Junc	.	9 27	56·2
11·3	Cargill	.	13 18	64·0
13·6	Burrelton	. .	15 10	68·0
15·8	COUPAR ANGUS		17 10	72·0
18·3	Ardler	. .	19 20	69·2
20·5	Alyth Junc	.	21 13	70·0
24·6	Eassie	.	24 43	70·2
26·8	Glamis	. .	26 38	66·0
29·6	*Kirriemuir Junc*		29 00	71·2
32·5	FORFAR	.	32 05	

goodwill—as popular on the footplate as he was in the board room.

Before closing the account of the Drummond prelude I must mention a splendid run made by one of these engines on the down 'Tourist' express in 1896, when No 61 took over haulage of that train at Perth, and essayed the 61 mph start-to-stop booking onwards to Forfar. She was making an extraordinarily good job of it, and after a fast climb to Stanley went on to average exactly 70 mph over the 18.6 miles from Cargill to Kirriemuir Junction. Here was another case of remarkable running on dead level track. Whereas these engines and the Lambies had been running at 75 mph on level track with the light racing trains of 1895, here was No 61 averaging 70 mph for nearly twenty miles on end with a load of 145 tons. Drummond had indeed scored a great success with these engines.

Front view of the record-breaking 4—4—0 No 17 with Driver John Soutar alongside

CHAPTER 2

'DUNALASTAIR I'

It is interesting to speculate upon how Caledonian locomotive practice would have developed had Dugald Drummond remained at St Rollox. A very high degree of efficiency had been attained in the '60' class 4—4—0s of 1882, and particularly so in those members of the class temporarily fitted with boilers carrying a pressure of 200 psi. Lambie made no more than minor changes in his new engines of 1895, and he maintained the very economical performance standards that had been established with the Drummonds. A test was made with one of them on the West Coast 'Corridor' trains between Glasgow and Carlisle which gave the following results:

GLASGOW—CARLISLE AND BACK

Train	2 pm UP	8.35 pm DOWN
Load, coaches	9	8
„ gross trailing tons	235	212
Number of stops	none	one
Lgth of run between stops	102·3 miles	38·7 miles
		61·6 miles*
Av speed between stops	45·5 mph	54·2 mph
		45·2 mph

Consumptions, round trip	
Coal per train mile	35·02 lb
Water per train mile	26·3 gall
Water evaporated per lb of coal	7·51 lb
Coal per net ton mile	0·18 lb
Coal per gross ton mile	0·13 lb

* Run from Beattock to Eglinton St

It is remarkable, first of all, to see that the Lambie engine hauled a load of 235 tons from Glasgow to Carlisle without assistance, including the long ascent from Uddingston to Craigenhill summit. The schedule even in Lambie days was the same as that worked by the big McIntosh 4—6—0 *Cardean* for many years after, albeit with much heavier loads, namely 135 min non-stop from Glasgow Central to Carlisle. In the reverse direction the little engine ran from Carlisle to the stop at Beattock in 44 min—again the same timing as that worked throughout, until the decelerations enforced in World War I. For such heavy work the coal consumption was notably low, at 35 lb per train mile on the round trip from Glasgow to Carlisle and back. In publishing details of these tests, and working out many items of performance relating to them *The Engineer* was moved to comment, in May 1895:

'Assuming that the coal burned costs the railway company 10s per ton in the firebox, we see that the cost of fuel for hauling the train 103 miles is 16s. We commend this fact to the advocates of electricity as a hauling agent. It is evident, we think, that whatever the advantages of the electrical system may be, it cannot possibly compete with the modern locomotive as far as cost of fuel is concerned.'

The present reader, and indeed railway managements of today must look back a little wistfully to a time when locomotive fuel cost no more than 10s a ton in the firebox. But apart from the costs of fuel, and the startling comparison it affords with the conditions of today, the performance of the locomotive was a very fine one, and demonstrates most forcibly the healthy state of affairs that existed on the Caledonian when McIntosh took office. He had a magnificent foundation to work upon, yet his development of design at St Rollox soon began to take a decidedly different turn. Although the racing trains of 1895 were light, and many of the ordinary express services loaded to little more than 100 tons, the portents for the future were different. Heavy bogie corridor coaches were coming into regular use. Dining and sleeping cars were included in the Anglo-Scottish trains, and the speed contest of 1895 was succeeded by a competition in amenities. McIntosh, as a running man, desired above all to

B

John Farquharson McIntosh,
locomotive superintendent, 1895 to 1914

So he set the St Rollox drawing office to produce a greatly enlarged version of the Lambie engine. The front-end was virtually unchanged, with a small increase in cylinder diameter from 18 in to $18\frac{1}{4}$ in; but the boiler, although of generally similar design, was much larger.

4—4—0 LOCOMOTIVE BOILERS

Engine, class	Lambie	'721'
Boiler:		
Tube heating surface	1071·5 sq ft	1284·45 sq ft
Firebox heating surface	112·65 sq ft	118·78 sq ft
Total heating surface	1184·12 sq ft	1403·23 sq ft
Grate area	19·5 sq ft	20·63 sq ft
Tubes:		
Number	238	265
External diameter	$1\frac{5}{8}$ in	$1\frac{3}{4}$ in
Lgth between tube plates	10 ft 7 in	10 ft 7 in
Barrel, mean outside dia	4 ft $6\frac{1}{4}$ in	4 ft $8\frac{3}{4}$ in
Height of centre line above rail level	7 ft 3 in	7 ft 9 in

The first engine of the new series, No 721, was named *Dunalastair*, after the estate of the chairman of the Caledonian Railway, J. C. Bunten. Such was the fame achieved by the new engines that this euphonious Scots name became a household word among British locomotive men, whether they worked in Scotland, England, India, Australia, or wherever engineers of British training took the standards and traditions of the home railways. But I could well imagine that however well the engines were known not one man in fifty could tell where Dunalastair itself was. In Scotland few locomotives have caught popular fancy to a greater extent than the first 'Dunalastair'. On paper the dimensions of the boiler, in comparison with that of the Lambies, does not suggest a vast increase; but the centre-line was pitched 6 in higher above rail level, and this,

have engines that would produce steam, freely. The Drummonds and the Lambies were excellent in this respect; but no refinements of front-end could make up for sheer steaming capacity in climbing gradients like the Beattock bank, like the southbound ascent to Craigenhill, like Dunblane, and like Gleneagles.

One of the first 'Dunalastairs', No 724

The pioneer engine, No 721 'Dunalastair', showing all characteristic features.
Driver J. Ranochan on the footplate

with the slight increase in outside diameter, resulted in a shortening of the chimney and dome, and gave the new engines a much more massive appearance. Technically they were a precise development of the Lambies, with the Drummond jacketed cylinders, direct Stephenson link motion and Vortex blastpipe, while the family likeness was accentuated by such details as the sandboxes mounted on the leading coupled wheel splasher, and the Drummond style of numberplate.

It goes almost without saying that they were magnificently finished in the dark Prussian blue, which was the official colour of all Caledonian passenger engines. The lighter blue, which was also so very attractive, will be referred to later. But the dark blue in association with the crimson lake of the footplate facings, steps, and tender underframes gave an immense character and dignity to the nineteenth century express locomotives. When blue

was adopted as the standard livery for the largest express passenger locomotives of the nationalised British Railways, and a shade not unlike that of the Caledonian decided upon, the beauty of former days in Scotland was no more than partially recaptured. The valences, steps and tender underframes were painted black, instead of crimson lake, and the blue, with nothing more than black, and white lining to set it off, lost much of its character. This BR livery did not last long, and the Great Western style which superseded the blue on the largest locomotives was more generally suitable than the halfway-house towards the full Caledonian style of old. Full details of the painting are contained in one of the appendixes, but so far as the 'Dunalastairs' are concerned, these engines did not at first carry the coat of arms on the tender. The lettering was a plain C R, with a full stop midway between the two letters.

19

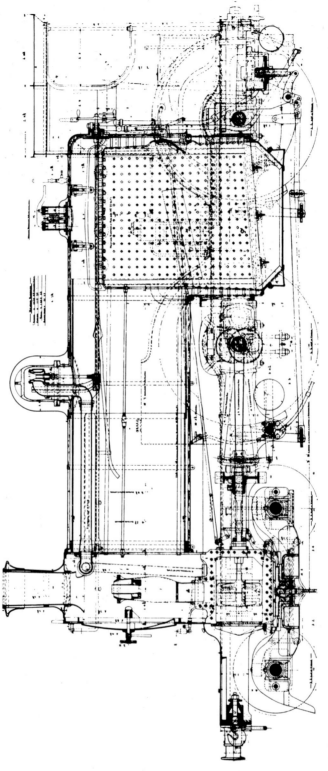

Reproduction of the official general arrangement of the 'Dunalastair I' class

Engine No 723 specially named 'Victoria' and used for Royal Train workings in Diamond Jubilee year

If the 'Dunalastairs' made a great impression upon members of the public, that welcome was mild compared to that which they received from the top-link enginemen. In Drummond and Lambie days it had, in modern popular parlance, been 'really something' to be an express driver on the Caledonian, and at joint stations like Perth and Carlisle it is to be feared that these great characters displayed a terrific superiority-complex towards their counterparts on other railways. Particularly was this so at Carlisle. All the Drummond 4—4—0s had their regular drivers, and no other, and of Tom Robinson—one of the heroes of the 1895 Race to the North—it was said that when he was in the Citadel station with engine No 78 he would hardly deign to acknowledge, let alone to fraternise with enginemen of other railways, even with his own allies in the Race, of the LNWR! In other respects Robinson was a great-hearted soul, but professional etiquette and pride took possession of him once he was on No 78! Many of the other Carlisle and Polmadie men were the same. They

had certainly engines to be proud of in 1895, and they justified that pride by their epic performances on the road.

Imagine then their feelings when the first 'Dunalastairs' arrived, to supersede the Lambies and Drummonds! Curiously enough Tom Robinson was one of the last drivers to get a 'Dunalastair' allocated to him, but all the fifteen engines of the class were in traffic and well run-in by the time the summer service—with the likelihood of another race—was introduced. The original allocation is shown (below) in the previous column.

The allocation of these fifteen 'super' locomotives in 1896 is in itself an interesting commentary upon the relative importance of the express train workings at that time, with four of them at Perth, six at Carlisle, and no more than three at Polmadie. Moreover, after No 721, which was immediately put on to the 2 pm Anglo-Scottish corridor trains, from Glasgow Central to Carlisle and back, it was not until four months later that Polmadie shed received any more of the class. Of the drivers, John Soutar who got No 724 made the record run from Perth to Aberdeen on the last night of the 1895 Race with the Lambie engine No 17, while Archie Crooks of Kingmoor had on the same night made the one and only non-stop run of the Race from Carlisle to Perth with a Drummond, No 90, and run himself so short of water in the process that having coupled off on arrival he refused to move further, and was towed to the shed!

The engines, although worked very hard while on the road, led a fairly sheltered existence so far as aggregate mileages were concerned. The Perth turns were, with one exception, typical, thus:

Engine No	Date completed	Shed	Driver
721	28/1/96	Polmadie	J. Ranochan
722	7/2/96	Perth	Will Hamilton
723	14/2/96	Perth	Andrew Brown
724	20/2/96	Perth	John Soutar
725	27/2/96	Perth	James Mitchell
726	9/3/96	Aberdeen	Harry Brown
727	18/3/96	Carlisle	T. Armstrong
728	30/3/96	Carlisle	T. Tervitt
729	3/4/96	Carlisle	A. Crooks
730	9/4/96	Carlisle	B. Johnston
731	16/4/96	Edinburgh	J. Dick
732	23/4/96	Carlisle	W. Lawson
733	30/4/96	Carlisle	T. Robinson
734	7/5/96	Polmadie	Andrew Dunn
735	14/5/96	Polmadie	John Bain

1. 9.10 am Perth to Glasgow
   A local run from Glasgow to Cumbernauld and back

5.30 pm Glasgow to Perth

2. 12.6 pm Perth to Glasgow
   5 pm Glasgow to Dundee and then Dundee to Perth

3. 4.4 pm Limited Mail, Perth to Carstairs
   10.24 pm Carstairs to Perth (Aberdeen portion of the down 'Corridor')

These three duties involved daily mileages of only 152½, 168½ and 155 respectively. By far the hardest of the Perth turns, and the hardest on the Caledonian Railway at the time, was the 8 pm sleeper to Carlisle, returning with the 2.17 am 'Tourist' express, a round trip of 302 miles in the night. On this duty, however, Perth alternated with Kingmoor and when on this duty the Perth engines and men had an easy day in between each long turn, consisting of no more than a single run to Dundee and back.

In that first year there was only one 'Dunalastair' working north of Perth, with engine No 726, from Aberdeen which ran the 5.40 pm down to Perth and then returned at 12.30 am with the down 'Corridor', a daily mileage of 180, but involving a very long time away from shed for the enginemen. This engine remained at Aberdeen throughout her existence. As LMSR No 14316, painted plain black, she was officially withdrawn in 1935; and when I rode the Midland compound booked for the up 'Granite City' in the summer of 1934, and with a heavy train we needed pilot assistance to Forfar, old 14316 was turned out to couple ahead of us and did some good work up the banks from Ferryhill and Stonehaven. Another interesting working was that of the one 'Dunalastair' allocated to Dalry Road, Edinburgh, No 731. At that time the Edinburgh sections of the morning Anglo-Scottish service by the West Coast Route were regarded as of equal, if not greater importance than those to and from Glasgow. Competition for the Edinburgh traffic from London had remained keen, even after the agreements following the Race of 1888; and there was, of course, the ever-present threat of the Midland competition. The 'M & NB' route was no party to the East Coast and the West Coast arrangements, and although the nature of the route largely precluded any equality in speed, the competition in comfort of rolling stock and in the beauty of the passing scene was keen enough.

Ever since the Race of 1888 the morning London-Edinburgh services by the West Coast Route had been given preferential treatment and for many years when division of the down express took place at Crewe the Edinburgh section preceded the Glasgow on the run northwards to Carlisle and Carstairs. The 'Dunalastair' engine No 731 was therefore put on to the 10.15 am from Princes Street to Carlisle, returning with the 4.30 pm. Both trains were non-stop over the 100·6 miles, and the scheduled times of 115 min southbound and 120 min northbound involved very strenuous average speeds of 52·5 and 50·3 mph respectively. The loads were not so heavy as on the afternoon 'Corridor' trains between Glasgow and Carlisle; but even so, the 10.15 am up from Edinburgh probably involved a greater output of power than the 45·5 mph of the 2 pm up from Glasgow. Apart from the very hard turn to Perth, with the down 'Tourist' express, the Carlisle 'Dunalastairs' ran the principal expresses to and from Glasgow, with the exception of the 'Corridors'.

Before passing on to some details of the magnificent performances these engines put up, almost from the moment of their introduction, some details of construction, though not peculiar to the 'Dunalastairs', may be mentioned. The frames were of 1 in steel plate weighing 2 tons 1 cwt each, as in the Lambies, and very strongly braced, while the generous proportions of the bearings contributed to the notable freedom from hot boxes that was enjoyed by Caledonian 4—4—0 engines in general. On the first 'Dunalastair' class the journal sizes were the same as on the Lambies, namely 8 in diameter by 7½ in long on the driving axle, and 7½ in diameter by 7½ in long on the trailing axle. The bogie was unusual in that the centre pin was 1 in ahead of the mid-point between the leading and trailing axles—thus 3 ft 2 in from leading axle to centre pin, and 3 ft 4 in to the trailing axle. The centre of the cylinders, which coincided with the centre line of the chimney, was at the mid-point between the two axles of the bogie.

As in the Drummonds and the Lambies, the steam passages were made very short and direct, while the pistons themselves were coned. The valve motion was designed in the old style, with short laps and short travel; but the 'Dunalastairs' provided a classic example of the truism, that one did not necessarily need to have long-lap, long-travel valves to secure a free running engine if the ports and steam passages were well designed. The valve motion details were:

Steam lap	1 in
Lead, in full forward gear	¼ in
Lead, in full backward gear	1/32 in
Travel, in full gear	4 5/16 in

With Stephenson's link motion the lead, in forward gear, would have increased still further as the gear was linked up, and the usual method of driving on

Another view of No 723 'Victoria', in which the handsome light-blue finish is evident

all the non-superheated 'Dunalastairs' was to work at about the fourth notch from mid-gear, out of a total of eight. The valves were set for approximately equal cut-offs at each end of the stroke in this position, and it was usual to fix the lever thereabouts and make all adjustments of power output on the regulator. Inevitably, however, there were variations between individual engines, and the drivers used to have little gadgets made whereby they could fix the levers between notches if necessary. On these engines, 'one notch' would mean almost 10 per cent difference in cut-off, and could make all the difference between successful and unsuccessful running. All Caledonian passenger engines right down to and including the Pickersgill 4—4—0s had lever reverse, and without these little personal gadgets they would have been susceptible to the disadvantage of coarse adjustment of cut-off. The only exceptions had been the Drummond 4—4—0s of the 1889 batch which had screw

reverse, and were run with much finer adjustments of cut-off.

From the days of Dugald Drummond the Caledonian standardised the Westinghouse air brake for all passenger-train workings; the pump was fixed on the right-hand side of the boiler, and the 15½ in diameter brake cylinder was immediately below the footplate with its centre line vertical. As originally built there was no hose connection on the front buffer beam. It was evidently intended that the 'Dunalastairs' would not need piloting. Later the hoses were added, but always hanging down, rather than embodied in the more usual vertical standpipe fitting. At the front all Caledonian engines were completely clear of upward projections. There were no lamp irons, and the whole area ahead of the smokebox door was flat and clear. Another characteristic fitting at the front was the long single-link coupling attached to the hook. It was frequently carried in the upward position

One of the Drummond 4—4—0s rebuilt with 'Dunalastair I' boiler : No 64

A 'Dunalastair I' No 733 on down West Coast express leaving Carlisle, and passing the south entrance to Kingmoor yard

leaning back against the top of the buffer beam. As on the North British Railway, only a part of the front buffer beam was in the traditional scarlet. The crimson lake of the footplate valences was carried around to include the mountings for the buffers, and it was only between the buffers that one found a scarlet panel.

Only four lamp irons were provided: one on each side of the cab; one in front of the chimney, for the semaphore head-code, and one on the back of the tender, for backwards running. The lamps on either side of the cab, like the port and starboard lights of a ship, indicated by their colours if the engine was approaching or receding. Seen from the front there was a white light on the right-hand side, and a green one on the left. Sometimes a lamp instead of a semaphore head-code was carried at the base of the chimney. There was another likeness to navigational practice on Caledonian engines in the splendid organ-pipe whistle, which gave such a distinctive deep-toned blast. Without having the

shrill note of the more usual bell whistles used on British railways, the Caley whistle had a great carrying power, and it was chosen for standardisation on the LMSR in Sir William Stanier's time. On the footplate, both Lambie and McIntosh retained the Drummond type of regulator handle, which instead of one long handle depending from the pivot boss was a straight lever pivoted at the centre, with a handle at each end. The regulator valve itself was of the double-beat type; that on the Caledonian dated from the time of Benjamin Conner.

The long-continued practice of allocating one engine to one driver resulted in the engines being kept in superb mechanical condition, while the paintwork was invariably immaculate. Drivers working on one engine only for months, and sometimes many years at a time were given to adding little touches of individual 'ownership'. One of the most popular forms of adornment permitted by the authorities was the fitting of ornamental surrounds to the base of the smokebox door handles. Engine No 732, stationed at Carlisle, ran for many years with a delicately-worked nine-pointed star on her smokebox, which she acquired in quite early days and was still carrying when W. J. Reynolds photographed her in Carlisle station in 1912. Other engines had an ornamental 'wheel' device like a steering helm of a ship, and individual enthusiasm extended to the fixing of something similar on to one of the little 'Jumbo' 0—6—0 goods engines. Two of the first 'Dunalastairs' were specially named and painted for Royal Train workings in the Diamond Jubilee year of 1897; these were 723 *Victoria* and 724 *Jubilee*. They were specially painted, and lined out in gilt and Royal purple, instead of the usual black and white lining. Both were Perth engines, and they worked Royal specials between Carlisle and Aberdeen in that memorable year.

The allocation of the first fifteen 'Dunalastairs' did not remain unchanged for very long in some cases, because with the building of the enlarged batch in 1897-8 many of the top workings went to the newer engines. Nos 728 and 729, for example, went from Carlisle to Dundee, and took over duties that until then had been run by Conner 7 ft 2—4—0s, as rebuilt by Drummond and Lambie. Again it was a case of individual allocation to drivers, and the men who had these two engines were W. Gellateley (728) and D. Mitchell (729). Of these men an old driver who knew them both well once wrote: 'It was aye said Mitchell saved his wages on the coal he used—for Will Gellateley's

A rebuilt Drummond 4—4—0 No 70 leaving Stirling with a Glasgow-Aberdeen express. This engine is running with a double-bogie tender

was aye blawing aff an black smoke a' ower the place. They were gey different as weel—Mitchell was gey quiet man, but Gellateley wis aye roarin' and sweerin' a' ower the place aboot somethin' or ither.' These two Dundee men each worked to Glasgow and back on two regular turns; local to Perth, in each case, and then the 7 am and 6.5 pm expresses to Glasgow.

When the time came for replacement of the original boilers of the Drummond 4—4—0s it was no more than natural to consider rebuilding the engines into the 'Dunalastair I' class. They had the same frames and wheelbase, and with successive reborings of the cylinders at overhaul there cannot have been much difference between the original Drummond 18 in cylinders and the 18¼ in cylinders of the 'Dunalastair I' class when new. In all, ten of the '60' class were rebuilt, as follows: Nos 60, 62, 63, 64, 65, 66, 70, 71, 73, and 75, at various dates between July 1898 and April 1902. The case histories of these engines is contained in one of the appendixes. There was another engine of which there is some doubt, namely No 84. The St Rollox records are somewhat vague on this, but a photograph exists showing the engine in service with a 'Dunalastair' boiler. Certain superficial changes

were made upon individual engines in the course of these rebuildings, including the fitting of modified cabs. When the original numbers were allocated to new Pickersgill engines from 1916 onwards the rebuilt Drummonds added 1000 to their numbers. As such they could perhaps have been regarded as on the duplicate list; but for traffic working purposes they were classed with the 'Dunalastair I' series, and did much excellent work. One of them, No 62, as LMSR No 14304 was not withdrawn until 1931, after a life of forty-eight years. Of the 'Dunalastair I' class proper the first to be withdrawn did not go until 1930, and the last one survived until the end of 1935.

Weight diagrams of the engines as running in 1918 show the following differences:

Class	Weight		
	Bogie	Driving	Trailing
	t c q	t c q	t c q
Lambie	14 - 13 - 2	15 - 7 - 3	15 - 4 - 0
Dunalastair I	15 - 14 - 3	16 - 0 - 0	15 - 5 - 0
Drummond rebuilt with Dun I boiler	15 - 3 - 1	16 - 0 - 0	14 - 17 - 3

The up West Coast corridor train at Glasgow Central with a Drummond 4—4—0 No 90 piloting a 'Dunalastair III'

CHAPTER 3

NEW STANDARDS OF PERFORMANCE

To appreciate the impact the 'Dunalastairs' made upon the railway world of 1896 one must reflect for a moment upon the position of eminence that the Caledonian Railway had earned for itself in the Race to the North in 1895. While there had been many heroic feats of individual running elsewhere, and examples of intrepid enginemanship on curving sections of line that came very near to the borderline of foolhardiness, so far as sheer engine *performance* was concerned the Caledonian must be considered to stand generally supreme. I have referred earlier in this book to the novel experience to be had behind the Drummond and Lambie engines of running at 75 mph sustained on level track, while the making of magnificent time between Carlisle and Beattock summit in the course of a run of 117·8 miles, non-stop, without any chance of replenishing the water supply was a tribute to the thermal efficiency of the engines concerned. The introduction, early in 1896, of new locomotives of markedly increased tractive power was bound to attract instant attention, and when it was learned that these engines were making much the same times between Carlisle and Beattock as prevailed during the Race, but with *double the loads,* can it be wondered that the connoisseurs of locomotive performance made long journeys through the night to Carlisle to witness such phenomenal work at first-hand. Nothing pleased J. F. McIntosh more than to have publicity for his new engines, and he was glad enough to grant footplate passes to enthusiasts like Charles Rous-Marten, Lord Monkswell, and the Rev W. J. Scott.

Even before *Dunalastair* herself was in regular express service Rous-Marten had a footplate trip in the company of McIntosh himself. The train was the down day mail, in February 1896, and from a standing start at Beattock station the performance was certainly most impressive. Weather conditions were perfect, but a gross load of 200 tons behind

the tender was a stiff proposition for an unassisted engine. I cannot do better than quote Rous-Marten's report of what happened, as contained in an article he contributed to *The Engineer* of 28 February 1896:

'Starting from Beattock, the line first rises two miles at 1 in 88, then two at 1 in 84, and finally six at 1 in 75 to the summit. This steep bank was ascended under easy steam, the regulator being only one-third open, and the reversing lever in the fourth notch. The steam pressure all the time was maintained just under blowing-off point. The lowest speed up the 1 in 75 was 25·7 m.h., but the engine was simply "playing with" the train, and working a long way within her powers. The summit—ten miles—was reached in 21 min 41 sec, and then, after a very steady descent of the two miles of 1 in 100, a short spurt was made down the length of easier falling gradient toward Lamington. The last three miles before this point were done at 73·8, 76·3, and 79·0 miles an hour respectively, and a still higher velocity would have been reached but for an aggravating check near Lamington, the train being a little before its due time, so that a preceding goods had not had time to get out of our way into a siding.'

Rous-Marten was much impressed by the steady running of the engine, and also its cleanliness on the footplate; but of course the engine was new, and conditions were ideal. Nevertheless, an equivalent drawbar horsepower of about 700, at so low a speed as 25·7 mph was a remarkable demonstration, under such manifestly easy working conditions. The cut-off in '4 notches' would have been about 35 per cent.

Lord Monkswell's first footplate experience on one of these engines was in July 1897, on the midnight Euston-Glasgow sleeper. He records that from the start that train, in Diamond Jubilee year, was hauled by the Webb compound *Greater Britain,*

'Dunalastair' 4—4—0 No 735 at Carlisle, waiting to take on a down West Coast express.
This photograph shows well the immaculate cleanliness maintained

then painted vermilion. He stayed awake during the night logging the run, and then at Carlisle boarded the 'Dunalastair' engine No 735. The load was relatively light, consisting of two sleepers, two ordinary eight-wheelers, and a six-wheeler—about 150 tons. They made a very fast run out to Beattock, passing Lockerbie, 25·7 miles, in 26 min 48 sec and Beattock station, 39·7 miles, in 39 min 53 sec. The Beattock bank was climbed in 14¼ min without speed falling below 30 mph, and some very easy downhill running followed, as the train was well before time by then. Despite a succession of checks after Symington, the train passed Carstairs, 73·5 miles, in 82½ min from Carlisle. But Lord Monkswell's comments are more interesting even than the fast times he recorded:

'I was most delighted with the engine. She ran very smoothly indeed, and the ease with which she brought the train along was quite absurd. Except at starting the lever was (all the while the regulator was open) in the 7th notch out of 17. The regulator was opened more or less according to the power wanted, but most of the time it was not half open. The fireman stoked comparatively little; he put on about 7 shovelfuls at a time mostly in the back of the firebox. The last 30 miles or so the fire was not touched. We started with the steam gauge at about 140 lbs. but the pressure soon rose to 160, and steam was blowing off all the first half of the way. The coal was mostly in fairly large lumps but there was some small stuff in it; it did not look of good quality at all, burning like wood. The firehole is fitted with a deflector which comes down so sharply, and when down is so near the fire that the driver has to hit it with a special handle each time the fireman stokes. When the deflector is down only about a foot and a half of the fire is visible.'

In referring to 17 notches of the reverser, Lord Monkswell is writing of the total number, from full forward to full backward gear. There were eight either side of the mid-gear notch, so that working in the seventh notch meant two notches from mid-gear, probably about 25 per cent cut-off.

Before coming to a critical analysis of their finest

work, on the down 'Tourist' express between Carlisle and Perth, two references to contemporary newspaper comment will indicate something of the tremendous impression these engines made upon the public generally. A correspondent writing to one of the daily papers and signing himself 'Admirer of C.R. Locos' described a run on the 2 pm up 'Corridor' from Edinburgh to Carlisle made on 11 January 1897, with a load 'equal to 12½'—that would be about 130 or 140 tons. The passing times were given as follows:

Princes Street	dep.	2.0	pm
Cobbinshaw	pass	2.25	pm
Symington	„	2.43	pm
Beattock Summit	„	3.9	pm
Carlisle	arr.	4.1	pm

There was evidently some very fast downhill running on this trip, though the engine was not extended uphill. There was no need to hurry after the very fine start to Cobbinshaw, which was passed 2 min early. In fact a minute was dropped on schedule between Symington and Beattock Summit. This correspondent claims a maximum of 87 mph down Beattock bank, and an average of 76½ mph from Ecclefechan to Gretna. The arrival in Carlisle 4 min early was made in spite of a long permanent way check south of Gretna and a slow approach to the station. The engine was the one 'Dunalastair' then stationed at Dalry Road, No 731, presumably in charge of her regular driver, J. Dick.

The second reference is a long newspaper cutting describing 'A fine ride on the footplate', with 'The Heaviest Train in England' (*sic*). All good Scots will be surprised to learn that this account relates to a run with the up 'Corridor', from Glasgow Central to Carlisle, with *Dunalastair* herself, and a load of 320 tons behind the tender. The full text of this account is printed on pages 35-37.

No 721 was double-headed to Carstairs, but after that covered the 73.5 miles to Carlisle in 84 min 53 sec, with no exceptionally high speed down the Beattock bank, and a maximum of 73 mph from Kirkpatrick down to Gretna. The date of this article is not quoted, but the indications are that it was published in the early summer of 1897. The only questionable point is a reference, during the ascent of Upper Clydesdale, to a boiler pressure of 175 psi. The normal figure on the 'Dunalastair I' class was 160 psi and this was duly noted by Lord Monkswell, on his trip with No 735 in the summer of 1897. It could be that No 721 had her pressure raised experimentally prior to the introduction of the 'Dunalastair II' class, which carried a pressure of 175 psi.

Now I come to the down 'Tourist' express, which in 1896 was booked to cover the 117.8 miles from Carlisle to Stirling in 125 min start-to-stop. There is no doubt that the small band of expert locomotive and train-running enthusiasts of the day 'cultivated' the crack Caledonian drivers, and encouraged them to show off the paces of their engines. In addition to Rous-Marten and the Rev W. J. Scott, who were both *persona gratia* with McIntosh himself, there was also A. C. W. Lowe, and the brothers Bell, who for so long owned *The Locomotive Magazine*. They became personal friends of drivers like Tom Robinson, Ranochan, Stavert of Dalry Road, and others; and these men, with their 'own engines' and an intense pride in their calling, delighted in showing what they could do. For this reason the early performances of the 'Dunalastairs' tend to stand considerably above what might have been expected had the stud been thrown into a 'common-user' pool to secure maximum utilisation. Their performances are period pieces as much as much in their background as in the trains worked and the loads conveyed. I must add, nevertheless, that such conditions persisted on the Caledonian throughout the McIntosh régime, and indeed right down to the time of grouping in many areas. The oft-quoted case of the 4—6—0 engine *Cardean* and Driver David Gibson on the afternoon 'Corridor' trains between Glasgow and Carlisle was perhaps an extreme example; but it symbolised a principle in locomotive allocation and manning which was prevalent in many parts of the Caledonian Railway in those spacious, and now far-off days.

I have tabulated herewith logs of two runs clocked by Rous-Marten on the down 'Tourist' express in the summer of 1896, which are as remarkable in the consistency of the times as in the intrinsic merit of the work done. In studying these logs it must be remembered that on the last night of the 1895 Race, A. Crooks with the Drummond engine No 90 and a load of 72 tons, had passed Beattock in 39½ min and cleared summit in 53 min; but he was running non-stop over the 150 miles from Carlisle to Perth and was nursing his engine not a little, to save water, and his time of 39½ min was not an indication of what an all-out time could have been. So far as the 'Dunalastairs' were concerned, one must note particularly the average speeds of 65.2 and 64 mph between Rockcliffe and Beattock station, made over a line where the average gradient is 1 in 580 against the engine. If one takes the modern figure for coach resistance, to arrive at a conservative estimate of the horsepower involved, these little engines were developing an average of about 500 equivalent drawbar horse-

THE DOWN 'TOURIST'
1.54 am CARLISLE—PERTH

Engine No Driver Load tons E/F		728 Robinson 161/170		733 Armstrong 170/180	
Dist miles		Actual m s	Av speed mph	Actual m s	Av speed mph
0·0	CARLISLE	0 00	—	0 00	—
4·1	Rockcliffe	5 03	48·7	4 59	49·4
6·1	Floriston	6 49	68·0	6 42	70·0
8·6	Greta Junction	8 58	69·7	8 53	68·6
13·1	Kirkpatrick	13 29	59·8	13 29	58·7
16·7	Kirtlebridge	17 21	56·0	17 17	56·8
20·1	Ecclefechan	20 36	62·7	20 31	63·0
25·8	LOCKERBIE	25 59	63·5	25 50	64·5
28·7	Nethercleugh	28 20	74·0	28 15	72·1
31·7	Dinwoodie	30 45	74·5	30 46	71·8
34·5	Wamphray	33 12	68·6	33 19	66·0
39·7	BEATTOCK	37 50	67·3	38 23	61·7
49·7	*Beattock Summit*	53 33	38·2	53 30	39·7
52·6	Elvanfoot	56 23	61·6	56 49	52·5
55·3	Crawford	58 36	73·3	58 57	75·5
57·8	Abington	60 36	75·0	60 57	75·0
63·2	Lamington	64 44	78·3	65 12	76·3
66·9	SYMINGTON	67 44	74·0	68 24	69·4
68·5	Thankerton	69 03	73·0	69 46	70·5
73·5	CARSTAIRS	72 46	80·3	73 40	76·8
80·7	Braidwood	81 00	52·4	81 40	54·0
84·0	Law Junction	83 49	70·3	84 29	70·3
89·9	Holytown	89 17	64·8	89 46	67·0
94·3	COATBRIDGE	94 13	53·5	94 29	56·0
109·7	LARBERT	109 22	61·0	110 11	58·8
117·8	STIRLING	116 53	—	117 40	—
2·9	Bridge of Allan	4 53	36·6	4 10	41·8
7·6	Kinbuck	11 17	44·0	10 26	45·2
17·2	CRIEFF JUNCTION*	21 12	58·1	20 45	55·9
19·3	Auchterarder	22 58	71·4	22 27	74·0
23·4	Dunning	26 27	70·7	25 47	73·8
33·0	PERTH	34 44	—	34 46	—

* Now Gleneagles

power over this length. The indicated horsepower was probably in the order of 750—a remarkably high figure for a small 4—4—0 locomotive of the 1896 vintage. These efforts were then substantially stepped up in the ascent of Beattock bank, where the average speeds over that gruelling ten miles were little less than 40 mph. The drawbar horsepower there, allowing for the loss of kinetic energy due to the fall in speed, works out at 800 in the case of engine No 733, and a little less for No 728. But in both cases the indicated horsepower must have been very near to 1,000—wonderful work for that period.

Both engines made very fast time down the Clyde valley, where the averages indicated maximum speeds of around 80 mph on both runs, and after the expected easing off due to the Carstairs slack,

and the rising gradients that follow the going once again became very lively onwards to Coatbridge. By Holytown both drivers were inside 'even time' from the Carlisle start. Then after the brief respite of the stop at Stirling and an opportunity to take water both drivers put their engines to it very hard up the Dunblane bank. Between Bridge of Allan and Kinbuck the gradient averages 1 in 100, and the average speeds of 44 and 45·2 mph would be close to the sustained speeds on that incline. The equivalent drawbar horsepower works out at about 850, a closely comparable effort to that on Beattock bank. The concluding work was smart, but without any exceptionally high speed down the bank from Auchterarder. Total running times of 151 min 37 sec and 152 min 26 sec over the 150·8 miles from Carlisle to Perth set entirely new standards of

'Dunalastair I' class 4—4—0 No 732 at Carlisle in 1912. This photograph is interesting as showing the tender without the coat of arms between the letters CR. This was the original style as shown on pages 14 and 18

express train running. Quite apart from any considerations of loads reckoned against times and speeds, the economy of the engines was no less meritorious. The tenders had a capacity of 3,570 gallons, and even if they had been completely full on leaving Carlisle they did not provide for the usage of more than 30 gallons per mile to Stirling, because the boiler had to be equally full at the latter place in readiness for the hard work needed up Dunblane bank.

Another train that attracted the attention of those early recorders was the most northerly 'lap' of the West Coast 'Postal' special, where it was booked to run the 89.8 miles from Perth to Aberdeen in 97 min. This train was normally not heavily loaded, and usually had no more than about 140 tons

behind the tender. The accompanying log was compiled by Rous-Marten, with an unspecified 'Dunalastair I' class engine. The start up to Stanley Junction was extremely vigorous, but after that relatively easy work was needed to keep time. In September 1898, Lord Monkswell footplated the train, and secured some considerably faster times, following a late arrival of the train at Stirling. He rode on one of the new 'Dunalastair II' class as far as Perth, and then transferred to No 726, the driver of which was then Philip Young. A signal check hindered the start, and made the time to Stanley Junction 9¾ min; but after that good time was made along the almost level stretch to Forfar. The lever was in the seventh notch, and the regulator less than half open, and speed ranged round 67 to 68 mph, rising to 73 mph near Glamis. The latter station, 26.8 miles, was passed in 27½ min, despite the initial check, and Forfar, 32 miles, was passed in exactly 'even time', at greatly reduced speed.

North of Forfar, Lord Monkswell did not record a great deal of intermediate detail; there were checks near Guthrie, and between Fordoun and Drumlithie, but it is evident that the engine was being worked under easy steam. The lever was as far back as the eighth notch for part of the way. Despite all the checks the train passed Cove Bay, 85 miles, in 85 min 55 sec; but a very cautious approach to Aberdeen made the final time of arrival 92 min 29 sec. In view of the lateness of the train harder running might have been made had not the driver suspected that one of the big ends was overheating. On arrival he found this was so; but Lord Monkswell gathered that No 726 was not

WEST COAST POSTAL SPECIAL
Load : 103 tons tare, 135 tons full
Engine : a 'Dunalastair I'

Dist miles		Actual m	s	Av speed mph
0.0	PERTH . . .	0	00	
7.2	Stanley Junc . .	8	51	48/8
11.3	Cargill . . .	12	56	60.1
20.5	Alyth Junc . .	21	31	64.3
32.5	FORFAR . . .	32	44	64.2
39.5	Guthrie . .	40	29	54.2
50.6	Dubton Junc .	52	40	54.7
66.5	Drumlithie . .	69	11	57.8
73.7	STONEHAVEN . .	76	48	56.8
89.5	Ticket Platform .	93	41	56.2
89.8	ABERDEEN . .	94	56	

At Crieff Junction, now Gleneagles : the up West Coast 'Postal' train, double-headed, passing a down train headed by a rebuilt Drummond 4—4—0 No 60

considered a very good engine at that time. She had been out of the shops two years, and was distinctly rough. In the circumstances it is perhaps a little surprising that the driver worked her at such short cut-offs as the eighth notch indicated. On another run with the postal train, with engine No 724 and Driver Soutar, the hero of the 1895 Race, the 89·8 miles were covered in 88½ min start to stop, but on Lord Monkswell's run, with a somewhat run-down engine, the net time cannot have been more than 90 min. The traditionally fast starts from Perth did not persist with the passing of the years, and later times of 10 to 11 min became usual. The same change took place at Carlisle, where more leisurely exits became the rule. Nevertheless, providing the regulator and lever were used judiciously there was nothing inherently wrong in making a brisk start. If the fire is well prepared, working at the same steam rate when starting as is to be maintained when running at full speed on the open road will yield much faster starts than those that have become hallowed by tradition on most lines. The Caley men who were passing Rockcliffe in less than 6 min from Carlisle with the down 'Tourist' were working much more nearly to the theoretically ideal. *

A very interesting record exists of the working of one of the Drummond engines rebuilt with 'Dunalastair' boiler. It was Christmas Eve 1903, and the 10 am London express from Glasgow Central was made up to '=15½', about 295 tons. Normally a stop was made at Strawfrank Junction to combine with the Edinburgh portion, but with holiday traffic the Glasgow section was to be run separately throughout to Carlisle. But evidently an engine failure took place at the last minute, and the only thing available for this crack working was No 18, a Lambie 4—4—0. This engine was obviously unfit for such a duty and began to lose time at once. Water had to be taken at the Motherwell stop; no rear-end banking assistance was available up to Garriongill, and after leaving Glasgow 4¾ min late the train came to rest at Strawfrank Junction in exactly 67 min from Glasgow, a loss of 22 min on schedule. Advice had evidently been sent to Carstairs to have another engine ready, and with the utmost promptitude a rebuilt Drummond, No 63, was substituted for the ailing Lambie. The process of engine changing took no more than 2 min 57 sec, and then there began the grand run tabulated herewith.

The log which was compiled by the late C. B. Ferguson of Curthwaite, near Carlisle, does not give details of the maximum speeds attained on the

Glasgow-Oban express near Glenboig, hauled by rebuilt Drummond 4—4—0 No 1075

One of the Drummond 4—4—0s rebuilt with 'Dunalastair' boiler, and renumbered 1070.
Photograph taken just after grouping

descents to Thankerton, and Lamington; but the minimum taking the intermediate rise to Symington was 43 mph. The maximum probably just exceeded 60 mph at the Clyde bridge beyond Lamington, and then an extraordinarily fine pace was maintained up the gradual rise to Elvanfoot. On the steep pitch just before that station speed fell to 40 mph, but recovered smartly on the brief stretch to the last Clyde bridge touching 46 mph. Then on

10.53 am STRAWFRANK JUNC—CARLISLE
Load : 9 coaches (=15½), 295 tons gross
Engine : Rebuilt Drummond 4—4—0 No 63

Dist miles		Sch min	Actual m s	Speed mph
0·0	*Strawfrank Junc* .	0	0 00	
4·7	Thankerton .		7 58	35·4
6·3	SYMINGTON .	9	10 07	44·7
10·0	Lamington . .		14 15	53·7
15·4	Abington . . .		20 19	53·5
17·9	Crawford . .		23 31	46·8
20·6	Elvanfoot . .		27 09	44·5
23·5	*Beattock Summit* .	30	31 25	40·8
33·5	BEATTOCK . .	40	40 25	66·7
38·7	Wamphray . .		44 39	73·7
41·5	Dinwoodie . .		47 03	70·1
47·4	LOCKERBIE . .	53	52 20	67·2
53·1	Ecclefechan . .		58 20	57·0
56·5	Kirtlebridge . .	62	61 08	72·9
60·1	Kirkpatrick . .		64 20	67·5
63·2	*Milepost 10* . .		66 57	71·0
67·1	Floriston . .		70 16	70·8
73·2	CARLISLE . .	80	76 55	

the final 2½ miles up to Beattock summit, on 1 in 99, speed fell away to 32 mph—no mean performance for a small 4—4—0 engine hauling almost 300 tons. To this point, not surprisingly in the circumstances, a little time had been dropped; but then the driver really went for it. Down Beattock bank speed was sustained at 75 to 76 mph for some distance, and it continued at 74 mph after Beattock station to the crossing of the river Annan. Fast running continued to Lockerbie, and then after a falling off on the rise to Castlemilk siding there was a fine finish. There is no record in the log of the maximum speed that produced the high average of 72·9 mph from Ecclefechan to Kirtlebridge but on the final descent towards Gretna the speed lay between 68 and 71½ mph for six miles on end. The result was a gain of 3 min on schedule time—a fine example of what the rebuilt Drummond could do.

Reverting to the 'Dunalastair I' class proper, their astonishing *début* on the 'Tourist' express was unhappily short-lived. On its very fast schedule of 125 min from Carlisle to Stirling it ran for no more than five months during the summer of 1896. There is no doubt that everyone concerned was keyed up ready for the resumption of racing against the East Coast, and with such engines as the 'Dunalastairs' at their disposal there is no knowing what record times the Caledonian drivers might not have achieved. But instead of a race there occurred the alarming derailment of this very train, at Preston, when two LNWR drivers, inexperienced in working it, took the curve at the north end of the station at

Engine No 724, formerly named 'Jubilee', as equipped for oil burning in 1912, during the prolonged coal strike of that year

nearer 50 mph than the prescribed 15 mph; and although the casualty list was extraordinarily small in the circumstances the accident sounded the death knell of really fast running on the night Anglo-Scottish expresses. The Caledonian was involved as much in the decelerations tabled in the winter of 1896 as any of the others, and the work of the 'Dunalastairs' and their larger successors thereafter became that of hauling ever-increasing train loads at moderately high speed.

Before leaving the 'Tourist' express, two other runs may be mentioned, which indicate something of the standards that were maintained in the summer of 1896. On one occasion when Rous-Marten was a passenger, engine No 728 was inadvertently supplied with coal of the wrong, and inferior, grade. The run was consequently classed as a 'failure'; yet on what was regarded as a poor run a load of 200 tons was taken from Carlisle to Stirling in 123 min—2 min *less* than schedule. It seems as though things were not considered satisfactory unless there was a gain of at least 6 or 7 min on schedule! On another occasion, once again with engine No 728 and Driver Robinson, the first 100 miles from the start had been covered in 97 min, and with little but favourable road left a truly record time to Stirling seemed possible. But a Royal 'horse-and-carriage' train was given priority at Larbert, and the 'Tourist' lost 12 min in consequence. Even despite this the arrival in Stirling was on time. Rous-Marten estimates that the net time on this outstanding journey was no more than 113 min. We can only rejoice that an enthusiast such as he was so frequently prepared to forgo his bed,

and clock the most exciting train, in what he himself described as 'the small—very small—hours of the early—very early—morning'! The performances of the 'Dunalastair' engines as thus documented form one of the most remarkable records of British locomotive performance in the nineteenth century.

Another very exciting duty worked by the 'Dunalastair I' class was not so fully documented. The engines stationed at Polmadie took their turns in working the Clyde coast flyers from Glasgow Central to Gourock. About the turn of the century competition between the Caledonian and the Glasgow & South Western for the traffic to the coastal resorts was at its zenith, and at one time the 4.8 pm from Central was scheduled to run the 26·2 miles to Gourock in 32 min. This was a very sharp timing having regard to the heavy slack required through Paisley, and the moderate speed demanded over the continuous curvature of the extension line from Greenock Central through Fort Matilda to Gourock pier. The train usually loaded up to about 200 tons, but the running, like that of the 'Tourist' from Carlisle, became something of a legend—so much so that some of the more sober-minded regular passengers demanded deceleration. Before the time got eased out to 35 min the regular drivers Keith Cowan, Joe Clark and Willie Short had made running that is still talked about among ex-Caley men in the Glasgow area. By a coincidence Cowan and Clark had namesakes on the Glasgow & South Western; but both the latter, although mighty runners, were Ayr men, and so did not work the rival boat train from St Enoch to Princes Pier.

A Newspaper Cutting of 1896

WEIGHT AND SPEED

The Heaviest Train in England.
A Fine Ride on the Footplate.

(By Our Own Expert.)

'Oh, waly, waly, up the bank,
And waly, waly, down the brae.'

Big as the Central Station, Glasgow, is, and long as are its platforms, the great train stretched well-nigh the station's full length, and the left-hand platform is 'throng' with farers and friends to see them off, with luggage-barrows and bicycles. For in five minutes the 2 p.m.—the 'London Diner'—starts, the heaviest of the many heavy trains which the Caledonian daily sends out of Glasgow, or takes on from Carlisle; in fact, its load (and that of its fellow, the 2 p.m. from Euston) is certainly the biggest of any express, perhaps of any passenger train, in this hemisphere, 'Nineteen-and-a-half' it is mystically said to be usually, which, being interpreted, should mean that it has the equivalent of nineteen and a half ordinary (6-wheel) coaches. At such times its load is 300 tons almost to an ounce. But today it has also an 8-wheel Cal-saloon for a family party, which means some twenty tons more.

Very tempting do its dining cars look, with their white napkins and glitter of glass and plate; pleasant also we know to be the walk along corridor and vestibule from end to end, even through intervening brake vans, and a chat with the friendly through guards; in fact, this train (like an even better one on the East Coast route) is quite 'the place to spend a happy day'. Not for us, however, are these delights; how the engines fulfil their heavy task is the thing to see, and the footplate the only place to see it. So we boldly say 'Loco Department' when asked for a ticket, and cotton-waste is in our hands instead of a dinner napkin.

THE START

Two engines for the first thirty miles of our journey; not really a 'pilot' the loco. foreman carefully explains, but just an engine working back home which can get back quicker than if sent 'light'; a small humpy little elderly goods engine, who doesn't look like pulling more than she can help. The other is No. 721, 'Dunalastair' herself, the eponym of that splendid class; by repute not quite so 'free' a goer as some of her sisters; for choice we would have liked 729 or 733 but they can all do splendid work. 'Do you know what you have on?' we ask; 'as good as twenty-one they tell me.' 'Yes, three "diners" (two London, one Liverpool), all 12-wheeled cars, nine West Coast corridor compos (8-wheelers), and one "Cally" saloon, a very good twenty-one too, for the weight is pretty close to 320 tons.' 'Pretty fair for one engine' says the loco-foreman, 'for they'll have but one after Carstairs.' 'Will they really do it with that load?' 'Ou ay, they'll do it right enough,' is the confident answer.

Hardly are we 'away' before we slip again, a train being in front of us on the very short section between the 'Central' and Bridge Street. With two engines on, however, we get into speed wonderfully fast, and when badly checked at Motherwell are before our time. (In the tangle of loops and branches a little south of Glasgow, the train keeps to the old main line by Motherwell, and not the slightly shorter Holytown loop). In consideration of the long incline in places fairly steep, which stretches, with some slight breaks, from the outskirts of Glasgow to within some five miles or so of Carstairs, the booked speed for the latter place is but moderate, so there is nothing surprising in our passing Cleghorn Junction three and a half minutes early. Approaching Carstairs, however, first comes a check, and then (just outside the station) a dead stop. The 'North'—i.e., Aberdeen—part of the dining train, which is joined with this at Preston, is late. 'Ah, she'll stop us again at Symington,' the driver laments, 'and it'll be a bad run.' We soon draw forward into the station, however, and are still a trifle to the good. The small helper, now back in its own stable, is soon uncoupled, but our big steed needs a drink. This takes up three minutes (3 min. 5 sec. to be exact) and it is 2.50.50, too, instead of 2.48—our 'schedule' time—when we are off again.

A LONG CLIMB

Now comes the really interesting part of the trip. There are some 600 ft. to be climbed in the next twenty-three and a half miles, without help from a bank engine. Though the average rise, including

A 'Dunalastair I', No 733, in the pale blue livery

some four miles of downhill, is easier than 1 in 200, the slopes are long, and the last pull to the summit as steep as 1 in 100. The full tender means nearly forty tons; the passengers, cooking stoves, and luggage, must mean another fifteen at the least; not less than 375 tons behind the footplate! We start without one slip of the wheels, or anything else to tell of the load that is being set in motion—luckily just at this point the gradient is favourable—and our second mile is run at over forty an hour. Lamington slips behind us in 9 min. 1 sec., and we look anxiously for Symington 'distant'; if that be against us, delay is our portion. But no, the Aberdeen train has taken up its Edinburgh part with unwonted quickness, and pressed forward out of reach, so all the signals are 'off', and in 11 min. 40 sec. Symington is safely passed.

Hitherto the 'lever'—these engines all have a real old-fashioned lever and notched quadrant, not any new-fangled reversing wheel—has mostly stood in the first notch from the middle; now it is shifted to and fro pretty often as the grades vary, the bank easing and then steepening again. We point to the gauge needle, and the fireman smiles; it quivers close to 175 lb. (the full pressure); plainly there will be no lack of steam to carry us to the top. But now comes Elvanfoot, in just over half an hour for the twenty-one and a half miles from Carstairs; the lever is put to the most forward point it reaches during the run, viz., midway between the second and third notches, and the regulator stands four-fifths open, for the next two miles are at 1 in 100 up. Tug, tug, tug, the pull is felt throughout the train, but the engine seems nowise distressed, and the speed keeps above thirty an hour.

Watch the time between each quarter-mile post

—27 sec., 27 3-5 sec., 28 sec.—that last is the slowest (better than thirty-two an hour) until the very last one, as we round the corner to 'Summit' Box, the many wheels of the long train grind against the curving rails and the quarter to the fiftieth mile post takes 32 2-5 sec. More than a thousand feet above sea level, a little-used high road at one side, and the lonely, wild, but lovely moor all round—why is this weird summit beautiful in all weathers, while Shap, so like it in so many ways, always strikes one as merely desolate and 'sullen'? the passengers sip their after-lunch coffee, and few of them think of the many thousand 'foot-pounds' of work done to lift them, their food, and their attendants, to this altitude. Thirty-five minutes ten seconds from Carstairs; a good forty an hour, inclusive, with the start thrown in; not many goods trains beat that on a level stretch, and our load, remember, is that of a goods, and a fairly heavy goods, too, and this is a section on which goods trains are nearly always helped by a 'bank' engine.

DOWN AND LEVEL

Now followed ten miles of steep fall, and we wind down rocky cuttings among wooded slopes through beautiful country to Beattock. If this bit were only straight, and had a rise at the end—but as things are, no time may be made up on it. A mile a minute pace is soon reached, but then ss-s, sss-s, goes the trusty 'Westinghouse', and the speed drops; again and again is this repeated until the last bend is reached, and Beattock Station is before us. Then the regulator is opened to about half way, and we spin at a great pace past that station, and along the lessening fall towards Locker-bie. Exactly 11 min. for the 10 miles from 'summit', cautious running where care is needed; now our engine is given 'its head' a bit, and we whirl past Lockerbie in 59 min., from Carstairs, the slight rise as the former station is neared, and a more decided one about Kirtlebridge being taken in our stride, as it were, and down the 1 in 200 bank past Gretna the miles take about 48 sec. each. Now, however, comes a final test; nearly six miles almost level, but with a slightly upward trend. As the impetus from the downhill run spends itself, the miles take 58 sec. and 59 sec.; then comes a mile of decided though easy rise, and we take 64 sec. over it. 'Give her a bit more steam,' we say, for the economical driver has his regulator not half open, 'there's a bit of a bank here.' 'We're ower it by now,' he answers, but shifts the handle an inch or so forward, and the effect is felt at once. The next mile takes but 60 1-5 sec., a rise in speed, which with such a load behind is truly wonderful.

TO TIME

Now 'bonnie Ca'lisle' is in sight; with a clear road we spin on at sixty an hour to within 600 yards of Citadel station, and without a jolt we pull up half way along the main up platform. Due at 4.15 p.m., it is not quite 4.16. That is, with a slip of one minute at signals, two bad signal checks, and a detention of over three minutes in Carstairs Station (where we were booked only to pass slowly) less than a minute has been dropped. But for the seventy-three and a half miles with one engine only we have taken 84 min. 53 sec. as against the 87 min. scheduled to us; a speed from start to stop of just over 52 miles an hour. We condoled with the fireman at starting, but he has worked no harder

than one has seen firemen on other lines work with less than half such a load behind them, and there is plenty of coal left for the return trip; the work has not only been done, but done with manifest ease. 'How many coaches do you think you could take, if you pressed your engine hard?' we asked; but this the driver of 721 won't undertake to say. 'All I know is, that we've never had our load yet.' The London and North Western, at any rate, were not inclined to take on the same load. At Carlisle the train was split up, the Liverpool and Manchester coaches going forward, with one engine, and the main London train following, with two 'diners' and five other vehicles—about 180 tons—and two engines as far as Shap Summit.

Last year we told how one engine of the same class ran 118 miles in as many minutes on a hard route, and a sister one covered four level miles (a shade of rise in fact) at over seventy-six an hour; even 'the rail-faring fool' could see that these were remarkable performances. But this last, which from a locomotive point of view, is perhaps, an even finer bit of work, is not at once so striking to the everyday reader. Well, let those of them who are wheelmen ride a fairly high-geared machine from Farnham over the Hog's Back to Guildford, or from Whitby up the long bank on the Scarborough road to the top of the moors—of course they can do either easily. Yes, but let them try it again with a luggage-cart hitched on behind their bicycle. We hope, permissu superidium, to further investigate the capabilities of these 'Dunalastair' engines; thus far, we can only quote McAndrews in 'The Seven Seas', and say with him:

Eh, Lord! they're grand—they're grand!

CHAPTER 4

THE 'DUNALASTAIR II' CLASS

THE success of the 'Dunalastairs' of 1896, and the advance in tractive capacity that they showed over existing engines, could well have led the locomotive department of the Caledonian Railway into a policy of standardisation, when authority was given for the construction of further new express passenger engines. But in 1897 and again in 1899 successive enlargements of the 'Dunalastairs' were made. At the same time, although the basic principles that had contributed so markedly to the success of the original engines were retained—namely, a very free-steaming boiler, and an excellent design of cylinders—in certain details there were changes. The increase in the cylinder diameter from $18\frac{1}{4}$ to 19 in left no room for the provision of a steam jacket round the cylinders, and this feature of Drummond design was therefore abandoned. The standard McIntosh fore-end, as originating on the 'Dunalastair II' class, was fitted to all saturated 4—4—0s from 1897 onwards and also to the '55', '908' and '918' classes of 4—6—0. Another change on the 'Dunalastair II' was the substitution of a plain blastpipe for the Vortex type; but the diameter of the orifice, $5\frac{1}{4}$ in, was large in relation to the cylinder volume, and ensured a free exhaust. The massive appearance, together with grace of outline that had so distinguished the first 'Dunalastairs', was enhanced in the '766' class, though the diameter of the boiler barrel, and the height of its centre line above rail level remained unchanged.

The distance between the bogie centre line and the leading pair of coupled wheels was increased by 1 ft, from 9 ft 11 in to 10 ft 11 in, to permit of a longer boiler barrel. The disposition of the tubes was the same in both the older and the newer engines, with 265 tubes of $1\frac{1}{4}$ in outside diameter; but on the later engines the distance between the tube plates was 11 ft $4\frac{1}{2}$ in against 10 ft 7 in. The firebox was the same on both series. The increase

in total heating surface, from 1403·23 to 1500 sq ft, was obtained entirely by the lengthening of the barrel. The power of the newer engines was increased by raising the boiler pressure from 160 to 175 psi as well as by the increase in cylinder diameter. Outwardly the look of the new engines differed slightly, because of a taller dome cover, standing 2 ft 6 in above the top line of the boiler, against 2 ft $4\frac{3}{4}$ in. It is extraordinary how so slight a change could be definitely noticeable. The chimneys were exactly the same. A further point was the removal of the sandboxes to the underside of the running plate. This certainly improved the already beautiful appearance of the 'Dunalastairs' in general.

The most prominent change from the first series of 'Dunalastairs' was in the tender, in which McIntosh introduced for the first time the large bogie type that was to be used on all Caledonian express passenger engines until Pickersgill's time. In these very distinctive and handsomely styled tenders the water capacity was increased from 3,500 to 4,125 gallons, in anticipation of the heavier work likely to be involved with increasing train loads on the long non-stop runs scheduled with many of the principal trains. With the average speeds substantially reduced as from the autumn of 1896, all the attention of St Rollox works was henceforth devoted to means for the conveyance of heavier loads. It would undoubtedly be a considerable advantage if long through workings like those between Carlisle and Perth could be made without taking water intermediately. The coal capacity of the original bogie tenders was described as '$4\frac{1}{2}$ tons without heaping'. The combination of the slightly longer engine with the bogie tender still further raised the Caledonian Railway in popular esteem, and in February 1898 Rous-Marten wrote: 'Their appearance at the head of a train at the Central Station, Glasgow, is always the signal for a large crowd to

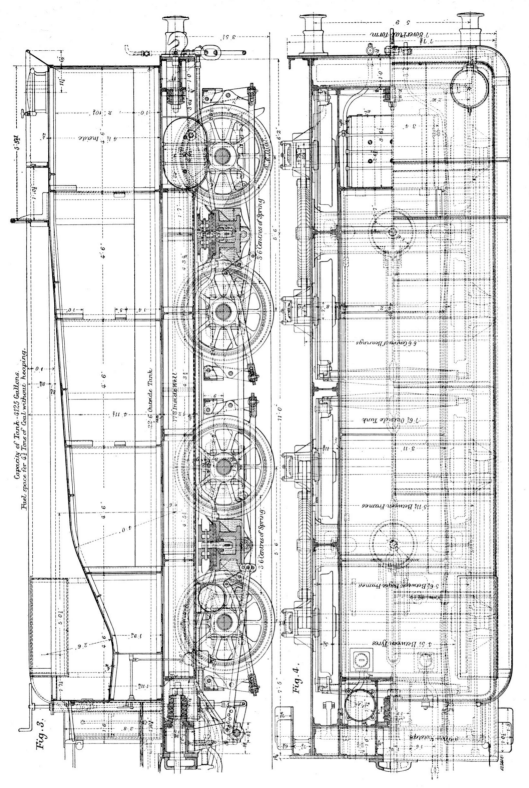

McIntosh's great bogie tender. This is the design used on the 'Dunalastair III' class. That used on the 'II' was longer, with a distance of 11 ft 3 in between bogie centres, but otherwise the same

The first engine of the second 'Dunalastair' class, No 766, before b...

assemble; indeed, on each occasion when I was present the engine was absolutely mobbed by admiring spectators.'

As in the case of the original 'Dunalastairs' the enlarged variety was built in a batch of fifteen, commencing with engine No 766 in December 1897. The last of this series, No 780, was completed at St Rollox in April 1898. They were designed for hard slogging work, and a most significant change from the original engines was a marked increase in the dimensions of the coupled wheel bearings. The Caledonian freedom from trouble with hot boxes can no doubt be attributed to the generous size of the journals:

CALEDONIAN 4—4—0 BEARINGS

Class	Driving		Trailing	
	Diameter	Length	Diameter	Length
'721'	8 in	7½ in	7½ in	7½ in
'766'	8½ in	7½ in	7¾ in	9 in

The weight diagram of the '766' class shows 16 tons 6 cwt; 16 tons 17 cwt; and 15 tons 17 cwt on the bogie, driving and trailing coupled axles respectively, compared with corresponding figures of 15 tons 14 cwt 3 qr; 16 tons 0 cwt 0 qr; and 15 tons 5 cwt for the '721' class. After a short time No 766 was named *Dunalastair 2nd*, while No 779 was named *Breadalbane*. For a time the class was generally known as the 'Breadalbanes' but when further developments of these already famous engines came in 1899 it became usual to refer to the '766' class as 'Dunalastair II', just as the appelation 'Dunalastair III' and 'Dunalastair IV' was used for the '900' and '140' classes.

Within weeks of the first introduction of the 'Dunalastair II' class Charles Rous-Marten was in Scotland riding on their footplates. The first two engines, 766 and 767, were stationed at Polmadie and No 766 was soon allocated to the afternoon west coast 'Corridor' trains, working to Carlisle and back as a single-home turn. On the relatively easy timing of 135 min non-stop from Glasgow Central to Carlisle the engine took a load of 330 tons tare without any assistance. After an excellent start speed rose to 60 mph on the brief descent to the crossing of the Clyde near Uddingston, and then on the long ascent to Craigenhill summit speed at no time fell below 30 mph. Although the gradients here are in no place steeper than 1 in 100 the climb is more than fifteen miles long. Furthermore, this was a mid-winter occasion, and Rous-Marten

ed, posed with the ancient 2—2—2 tank engine No 1A at St Rollox

records that a strong westerly wind was blowing throughout the journey. Carstairs was passed in 47 min for the 29 miles from Glasgow—a minute early; but after that the journey was hindered by the presence of the Edinburgh section of the train only just ahead. There was a signal stop at Symington, and although the subsequent recovery was good the train was nearly 4 min late passing Beattock summit, in 80 min 51 sec from Glasgow. The rest was nevertheless easy. Running under easy steam, and not exceeding 75 mph on the steepest falling gradients, the 49·7 miles to Carlisle were covered in 50 min 55 sec from Glasgow.

Before referring to Rous-Marten's return trip to Glasgow on the down 'Corridor', an important test run on the 2 pm up 'Corridor' with engine No 772 needs special mention. The particular engine was almost brand new at the time; she was completed at St Rollox on 1 February 1898, and this test run was made on the twenty-third of the same month. The tare load of 305 tons behind the tender indicated one coach less than on Rous-Marten's footplate trip with No 766, but the running was virtually unchecked until nearing Lockerbie. Very comprehensive details of the performance are given on a diagram prepared in the St Rollox drawing office and dated 5 May 1898. A reproduction of this diagram, taken from *The Engineer* of 23 December

1898, is included herewith. Very great interest is attached to the working of the engine on the long and arduous ascent from Uddingston to Craigenhill box, and certain details have been extracted from the diagram for ready reference. Regulator openings, for example, can be misleading if related purely to the position of the handle on the quadrant plate, and on the great majority of locomotives steam chest pressure gauges were not fitted until the time of Gresley. On this diagram the actual area of the regulator opening is given. It will be noted that the boiler was blowing off at 180 psi, 5 lb higher than the nominal pressure of the 'Dunalastair II' class.

The opening out from 31 to 38 per cent cut-off at Wishaw seemed to 'beat the boiler', because soon after Law Junction was passed the pressure began to fall, and as the diagram shows it rallied rather slowly even with the period of easy working after Cleghorn, with the regulator completely shut for a distance of about 3 miles approaching Carstairs. Even so, it must be conceded that the development of an indicated horsepower of almost 1,000 at speeds of 27 to 30 mph represented most remarkable work for an engine of these dimensions. The second stage of the ascent to Beattock summit was taken much more easily. Cut-off was 31 per cent all the way, and the regulator openings varied from 34 to 78 per cent of the maximum area until the train

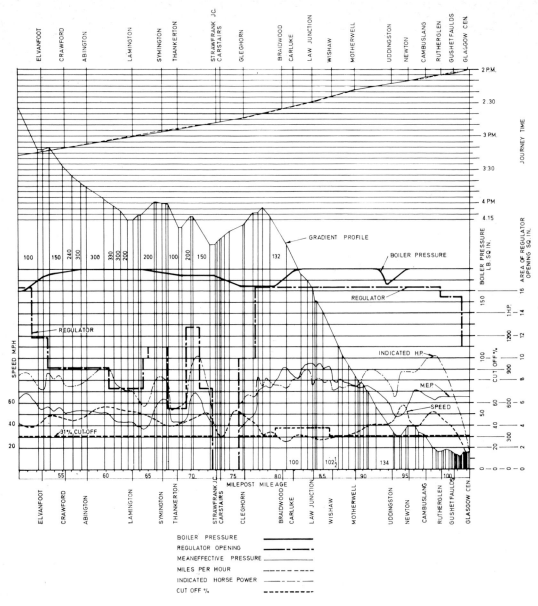

TRIAL RUN : 23 FEBRUARY 1898

2 pm CORRIDOR DINING TRAIN, GLASGOW TO CARLISLE

'Dunalastair II' class engine No 772

Weight of train, exclusive of engine and tender, 305 tons, 50 pairs of wheels. Total length of train 586 ft

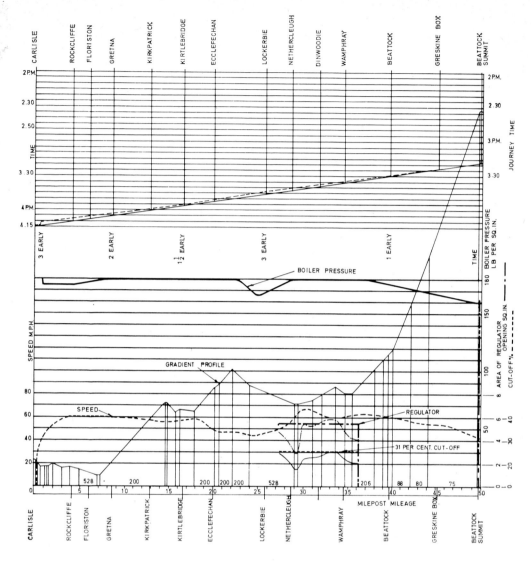

TRIAL : 23 FEBRUARY 1898

2 pm CORRIDOR DINING TRAIN, GLASGOW TO CARLISLE

'Dunalastair II' class engine No 772

Slacked for plate-layers after Cambuslang. No particulars taken after passing Nethercleugh owing to constant interruptions by signals

Water evaporated per mile 34·3 gallons

,,   ,,   ,, lb of coal 7 gallons

Total water evaporated 3,500 gallons

Temperature of water in tank 45 deg F

Coal consumed by gallon of water evaporated 1·44 lb

Engine No 772 on the test run described, with a very rough-and-ready indicator shelter at the front end

was above Elvanfoot, when there was a short spell of full regulator working up to Beattock summit. By that time, however, the firing was being eased to avoid having too great a head of steam on passing the summit. Pressure was down to 160 psi, and the indicated horsepower on this last stage of the ascent was 880. The water consumption was 34·3 gallons per mile and the coal consumption almost exactly 50 lb per mile. For the period the coal consumption must be regarded as heavy, though not so in relation to the work done, or in relation to the grade of coal normally used on the Polmadie top-link jobs. The

average consumption was 112 lb per sq ft of grate area per hour, another heavy figure, particularly so as most of the coal would have been consumed in the first 80 min of the journey.

On Rous-Marten's return trip on the 'Corridor' the tare load was 276 tons, very little less than the standard minimum load of seven 12-wheelers taken in *Cardean*'s day. From the way he wrote it would seem to have been fully the intention to take this train up Beattock bank without assistance. They had certainly made a very fine start, passing Lockerbie, 25·8 miles, in 30 min 12 sec, and

CALEDONIAN RAILWAY : TEST OF ENGINE No 772

Location	Speed mph	Regulator opening	Cut-off %	Boiler pressure psi	Mean effective pressure psi	ihp
Rutherglen Junc	50	Full	31	180	65	1,020
Newton	40	Full	31	177	71	870
Uddingston	58	Full	31	167	47	660
Before Motherwell	40	Full	31	180	75	900
Flemington	30	Full	31	180	78	770
Garriongill Junc	27	Full	38	180	90	950
Law Junc	31	Full	38	180	90	950
Braidwood	26	Full	38	170	73	850

A beautiful picture of No 766 in light blue and named 'Dunalastair 2nd'

Wamphray, 34·5 miles, in 38 min 28 sec. The average speed between the last two places was 63·3 mph. But at Murthat box, signals were adverse, and the train was brought practically to a stand, having done the first 36 miles from Carlisle in exactly 40 min. Such a time naturally invites comparison with Great Western starts from Paddington out to Reading; but the Caledonian road with its lengthy stretches of 1 in 200 is much harder. This virtual start-to-stop average of 54 mph was thus an extremely fine achievement for the year 1898. But the stop at Murthat made it inexpedient to try and

tackle Beattock bank without help, particularly as it was a wet and windy evening. Rous-Marten does not give any details of the climb, but they went very smartly down to Strawfrank covering the 23·5 miles from Beattock summit to the stop in 20 min 49 sec, with stretches run at 78 and 80 mph. At that period the train called at Eglinton Street, and after detaching the Edinburgh portion at Strawfrank a very fast run was made downhill to the former station, $28\frac{1}{4}$ miles in 31 min 17 sec start to stop.

Lord Monkswell rode engine No 774 on the down 'Postal' between Stirling and Perth. He got an

Engine No 772 in light blue, original non-superheated condition. This engine was twice rebuilt in later years

excellent run, with a load of about 150 tons. In his diary he wrote: 'Before travelling on No 774 I had been rather inclined to sniff at the "Breadalbanes" as likely to be no real improvement on the "Dunalastairs", but a run on one of them soon put a stop to that! To begin with they are the most strikingly steady machines I have ever been on.' He continued:

'After starting, the reversing gear was put into the 4th notch with the regulator half open, and the firing was kept up practically continuously till we reached Kinbuck, at the top of the Dunblane bank. The effect of this was that when going through the tunnels near Bridge of Allan the chimney produced a fountain of sparks like the tail of a comet.'

Kinbuck, 7·6 miles, was passed in 11 min 40 sec and Crieff Junction, 17·2 miles, in 21 min 47 sec. Then, Lord Monkswell writes: '. . . a fairly swift descent of the hill into Perth took place, but steam was shut off at intervals to prevent the speed rising too high, so that no unusual pace was attained. The darkness of the morning and the low blowing steam from the engine itself prevented me timing all the miles, but one was certainly run at 75½ mph, while for a considerable distance none of the quarter miles which I did succeed in timing took more than 12 2/5 sec—72 mph. While descending the hill I was sitting on the seat in the front left-hand corner of the tender, where I got the best view of the mileposts, and also felt the full strength of the wind rushing past me. I have never experienced any more exhilarating feeling than that downhill rush through the cold morning air while it was still twilight.'

Signals checked their approach to Perth, but the total time from Stirling was 36 min 19 sec for the 33 miles.

Details of an excellent run on the 10.5 am up from Aberdeen to Perth, with engine No 775 are tabulated herewith. The figures were taken from an article in *Engineering* of 15 June 1900; but while very complete details are given of the running between Stonehaven and Dubton Junction, and again between Forfar and Perth, no intermediate times and speeds are quoted for the sections between Aberdeen and Stonehaven, or between Bridge of Dun and Forfar. Climbing the Fetteresso bank, out of Stonehaven, the gradients are very severe to milepost 222, on 1 in 85, 90 and 1 in 107. There is then an easing to 1 in 423, past Dunnottar signal-box, and it is here that speed must have risen to all but 50 mph to make an average of 43.3 mph from post 222 to 221; then there is the final pull at 1 in 102 up to milepost 220¼. On the many runs I recorded personally in the 1930s, with both LMS

and LNER engines over this route I found it rare to pass milepost 220¼ in less than 10 min, with loads that were lighter in relation to the tractive power of the locomotives, so that No 775 was doing extremely well here. She was then taken downhill with tremendous gusto, reaching a maximum speed of 82 mph on Marykirk bank, and making the fast start-to-stop time of 26½ min from Stonehaven to Dubton.

10.5 am ABERDEEN—PERTH

Load : six 8-wheelers; four 6-wheelers; 210 tons full
Engine : 4—4—0 No 775 (Dunalastair II class)

Dist miles		Actual m s	Av speed mph
0·0	ABERDEEN . . .	0 00	
16·1	Stonehaven . . .	22 25	
2·9	Milepost 222 . . .	6 25	—
3·9	,, 221 . . .	7 48	43·4
4·7	,, 220½ . . .	9 05	35·2
5·9	,, 219 . . .	10 50	42·8
6·9	,, 218 . . .	12 02	50·0
—	Drumlithie . . .	—	—
8·9	Milepost 216 . . .	13 58	62·0
10·9	,, 214 . . .	15 40	70·5
—	Fordoun . . .	—	—
11·9	Milepost 213 . . .	16 30	72·0
12·9	,, 212 . . .	17 21	70·5
13·9	,, 211 . . .	18 13	69·2
—	Laurencekirk . . .	—	—
15·9	Milepost 209 . . .	20 04	64/3
16·9	,, 208 . . .	20 55	70·5
—	Marykirk . . .	—	—
17·9	Milepost 207 . . .	21 44	73·4
—	Craigo . . .	—	—
19·9	Milepost 205 . . .	23 15	79·4
20·9	,, 204 . . .	24 05	72·0
21·9	Kinnaber Junc (203) .	23 58	67·9
23·1	DUBTON JUNCTION .	26 30	
2·7	Bridge of Dun . .	4 07	
15·4	FORFAR . . .	19 45	46·8
1·7	Milepost 182 . . .	3 27	—
3·7	,, 180 . . .	5 33	57·1
10·7	,, 173 . . .	11 53	64·6
—	ALYTH JUNCTION .	—	
12·7	Milepost 171 . . .	13 38	68·0
16·7	COUPAR ANGUS (167) .	17 06	69·2
		pws	30
20·7	Milepost 163 . . .	22 04	48·9
21·7	,, 162 . . .	23 06	58·0
22·7	,, 161 . . .	24 06	60·0
23·7	,, 160 . . .	25 06	60·0
24·7	,, 159 . . .	26 07	59·0
—	Stanley Junction . .	—	—
27·7	Milepost 156 . . .	28 44	69·0
—	Luncarty . . .	—	—
28·7	Milepost 155 . . .	29 32	75·0
29·7	,, 154 . . .	30 19	76·5
30·7	,, 153 . . .	31 07	75·0
31·7	,, 152 . . .	32 02	65·4
32·5	PERTH . . .	33 09	

Net time Forfar to Perth 31 min

Two 'Dunalastair II' 4—4—0s : No 779 'Breadalbane', and a second unidentified engine

The section from Bridge of Dun to Forfar was also smartly run, as this included the ascent of Farnell Road bank, $3\frac{1}{4}$ miles at 1 in 100-120, and level running elsewhere. Then finally came the sprint from Forfar to Perth. Here the start was brisk, and after Alyth Junction the speed remained very steady at 69 mph on the level until slowing was necessary for the permanent way slack beyond Coupar Angus. The succeeding section to Stanley Junction includes the sharply graded 'dip' to the crossing of the River Tay at milepost 162. The descent at 1 in 160 helped the acceleration from the slack, and on the mile of 1 in 140 rising beyond the average fell very little below 60 mph. Then once again the driver let the engine go for all she was worth down the final descent into Perth, touching $80\frac{1}{2}$ mph, and evidently not braking until

the very last minute. A time of 1 min 7 sec for the 0·8 mile from milepost 152 into the station certainly sounds venturesome today; but the Caledonian express drivers were past masters in the art of working the Westinghouse brake, and time was frequently gained, in complete safety, by these rapid approaches to stations.

Moving now to the southern end of the line, two runs on the up morning Liverpool and Manchester 'Scotsman', from Beattock to Carlisle show once again the speedworthiness of the 'Dunalastair II' class in their early days. These two runs were clocked within three days of each other, in September 1902, and on the unchecked sections were remarkable for the close correspondence of the running times, despite the difference in load. The downhill gradient from Beattock station—1 in 200

Liverpool and Manchester to Glasgow and Edinburgh express passing Kingmoor, hauled by engine No 769. The second and third vehicles in the train are L & YR stock

11.43 am BEATTOCK—CARLISLE

Engine: 'Dunalastair II' No . . . Load tons E/F		768 225/240		768 275/290	
Dist miles		Actual m s	Av speed mph	Actual m s	Av speed mph
0·0	BEATTOCK	0 00	—	0 00	—
5·2	Wamphray	6 41	46·7	6 40	46·8
8·0	Dinwoodie	9 15	65·5	9 20	63·1
11·0	Nethercleugh . . .	12 00	65·4	12 14	62·1
13·9	LOCKERBIE . . .	15 12		15 36	
5·7	Ecclefechan . . .	8 19	41·1	8 35	39·8
9·1	Kirtlebridge . . .	11 24	66·2	11 34	68·3
12·7	Kirkpatrick . . .	14 55	61·6	15 00	62·8
		sigs			
17·2	Gretna Junction . .	19 54	53·9	19 00	67·5
19·7	Floriston	22 36	55·5	20 55	77·8
21·7	Rockcliffe	24 44	56·2	22 56	59·6
25·8	Carlisle	29 31		27 25	

for more than three miles—is ideal for making a fast start; but the smart times to Lockerbie were once again helped by the rapid approaches to that station. The restart from Lockerbie is adverse for three miles, first on 1 in 528, and then including $1\frac{1}{2}$ miles at 1 in 200. It was thus excellent work for a 'Dunalastair II' to pass Ecclefechan in such times as 8 min 19 sec and 8 min 35 sec with these loads. On both occasions the engine was running freely downhill, and the average speeds indicate maxima over 70 mph at Kirtlebridge. But on the first run a signal check at Gretna spoiled the best running

12.40 pm CARLISLE—GLASGOW
Load : to Carstairs 11 8-wheelers 290 tons
to Glasgow 8 8-wheelers 215 tons
Engine : Dunalastair II class No 770

Dist miles		Sch min	Actual m s	Av sp mph
0·0	CARLISLE . .	0	0 00	—
8·6	Gretna Junc . .		11 51	
25·8	LOCKERBIE . .	29	33 20	48·0
39·7	BEATTOCK . .	43	48 21	
10·0	Summit . . .	18	19 53*	
27·2	Symington . .		37 28	58·6
33·8	CARSTAIRS . .	43	44 32	
10·5	Law Junction .	12	14 25	—
16·4	Holytown . .	20	20 50	55·3
21·0	Uddington . .	25	26 01	53·2
28·4	Eglinton St . .	37	35 42	
1·0	GLASGOW CEN .	4	3 38	

banked in rear

section of all, and caused a loss of $1\frac{3}{4}$ min to 2 min. On the second occasion the maximum speed at the Solway Firth must have been at least 80 mph, and once again, on both runs there is evidence of a very fast approach to Carlisle station by concluding times over the 4·1 miles in from Rockcliffe of 4 min 46 sec and 4 min 29 sec.

Another interesting run was logged by the late Edward Little, in August 1903, on the 12.40 pm down from Carlisle. This train was the 5.15 am 'Newspaper' express from Euston, and had its more recent equivalent in the 9.25 am departure from Crewe. In relation to its load this train was very sharply timed—too sharply for a 'Dunalastair II', with a load of 290 tons behind the tender—and as the accompanying log shows no less than $5\frac{1}{4}$ min was lost between Carlisle and Beattock. The allowance to passing summit was only 64 min, with a 3 min scheduled stop at Beattock. This compares with the down 'Corridor' timing of 66 min with 2 min allowed for attaching the bank engine. On this occasion the 12.40 pm was almost up to the weight of the 'Corridor'. The Beattock stop was cut to 1 min 10 sec, but even with a bank engine the optimistic 18 min allowed to climb the bank itself was exceeded by almost 2 min and having left Carlisle 5 min late, the train was thus $10\frac{1}{4}$ min late in passing summit.

The downhill speed was no more than ordinarily brisk on this occasion, and Carstairs was reached exactly 10 min late. It was the station staffs that did the time-cutting on this occasion, and the Carstairs men, who were allowed 8 min, saw the train away

'DUNALASTAIR II' PERFORMANCE

Run	Engine No	Load tons/tare	Dist miles	Time m s	Speed mph
Stirling-Perth	772	65	33·0	32 05	61·6
Stirling-Perth	774	65	33·0	32 45	60·4
Beattock-Carlisle . . .	772	218	39·7	41 15	57·7
Strawfrank-Carlisle . . .	772	255	73·2	78 00	56·2
Thankerton*-Carlisle . . .	767	329	68·5	83 35	49·3
Carlisle-Carstairs . . .	774	237	73·5	83 45†	52·6

* From signal stop   † Including slight signal checks

in 2 min 34 sec with a reduced load of 215 tons. A further minute was gained by engine on the downhill section, and Eglinton Street was reached only 3¼ min late. For once a 'Dunalastair II' did not seem to be in characteristic form on this occasion.

Further runs with the 'Dunalastair II' class engines made about the turn of the century are summarised in the accompanying table. One would like to have had more detail of the run with No 774, when she worked the down 'Postal' from Carlisle to Carstairs, with a load of 237 tons tare, and took no assistance up Beattock bank. The schedule time of this train was then 84 min and it was probably the hardest all-the-year-round task set to Caledonian engines after the summer 'Tourist' express had been decelerated. On this occasion there was an observer on the footplate, and he noted that the ten miles of the bank were climbed in 18¼ min, with a minimum speed of 27½ mph. This of course was very hard work, and the boiler pressure had dropped to 150 psi at the summit.

The lightly loaded runs from Stirling to Perth were made with the down 'Postal', and although they do not involve any great output of power the

STIRLING—PERTH : THE DOWN 'POSTAL'

Load : 3 coaches, 65 tons tare
Engine : 'Dunalastair II' class No 772

Dist miles		Actual m s	Av speed mph
0·0	STIRLING . .	0 00	—
2·9	Bridge of Allan . .	4 03	43·0
4·9	Dunblane . .	6 22	51·9
7·6	Kinbuck . .	9 30	51·7
10·8	Greenloaning . .	12 45	59·1
15·0	Blackford . .	16 23	69·2
17·2	Crieff Junction . .	18 35	60·0
19·3	Auchterarder . .	20 10	79·5
23·4	Dunning . .	23 30	74·0
26·2	Forteviot . .	25 48	73·1
29·1	Forgandenny . .	28 02	77·7
31·0	*Hilton Junction* . .	29 30	77·7
32·0	*Friarton Box* . .	30 35	
33·0	PERTH . .	32 05	

complete details of the first of the two, that with engine No 772, provide a most interesting 'period piece' in express train working in 1899-1900. The log is tabulated herewith. The speed was never less

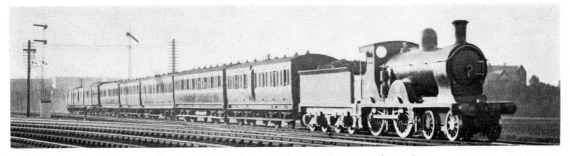

Engine No 775 nearing Carlisle, with up stopping train

Engine No 770 in original dark blue livery

than 50 mph up Dunblane bank, and some fast time was made up the rising stretch to Gleneagles summit. Then a free run downhill and the usual lightning finish produced a start-to-stop average speed of 61·6 mph.

Despite these records of excellent work, old Caledonian men have told me that the 'Dunalastair II' class never quite attained the same degree of popularity enjoyed by their predecessors. They were of course followed very shortly by the '900' class, which in many respects were among the most outstanding of the whole family both in the artistry of their external design, and in their immaculate performance. But the 'Dunalastair II' class have one claim to celebrity that places them above all the others, namely that McIntosh was approached by the Belgian Government of the day to supply some similar engines for service in Belgium. This most interesting episode is referred to in Caledonian archives as follows:

Extract from Minutes of Meeting of the Traffic Committee.
Glasgow, 8th. February 1898.
Belgian State Railways and "Dunalastair" class of Engine.
Submitted letter from Mr. McIntosh with translation from a communication from the Chief Engineer of the Belgian State Railways.

Remit to Board.
Extract from Minutes of Meeting of the Board of Directors.
Glasgow, 8th. February 1898.
Belgian State Railways and "Dunalastair" class of Engine.
Submitted letter from Mr. McIntosh with translation from a communication from the Chief Engineer of the Belgian State Railways.

Remit to Chairman to authorize Mr. McIntosh to give to the Belgian Government drawings and full particulars for 5 engines of the Dunalastair

The first of the Belgian 'Dunalastairs' photographed at the works of Neilson, Reid & Co with Mr McIntosh standing in front

type and to endeavour to arrange for their being built in Glasgow under the special supervision of a Locomotive Engineer to be selected by Mr. McIntosh, who in respect of the very special circumstances is notwithstanding the terms of his engagement with the Company authorized to undertake a general supervision of the construction of the 5 engines.

James C. Bunten.

There were certainly a number of differences in detail between the Scottish and the Belgian 'Dunalastairs', the most noticeable of which was the change to right-hand drive, in accordance with standard Belgian practice. I have had an opportunity of studying correspondence that took place between the St Rollox drawing office and Messrs Neilson Reid & Co, and quite apart from the actual detail points raised and discussed in this correspondence it is interesting to find it is all handwritten between the engineers concerned on either side: R. W. Urie and T. Weir of the Caledonian Railway, and Messrs Snowball and Wilson of the contractors. There is a long letter, written by a clerk and signed by J. F. McIntosh personally, concerning the painting, which concludes: 'I will send my Foreman Painter to your works later on, before the engines are painted and lined, to show you our practice, particularly in regard to the lining.' Belgian engines were then normally painted black with red lining, but not so the 'Dunalastairs'.

In *The Railway Magazine* for September 1899 there was an article 'Through Belgium by Rail' in which the author has the following comment to make:

A 'Dunalastair' at Antwerp, Belgian State Railways

'When I got on the platform at Antwerp of course I strolled down to have a look at the engine that was to haul us, and there, lo and behold, was a familiar dark blue locomotive that made me think for a second I had reached Scotland by mistake, and had come upon the famous "Dunalastair". One official turned up his eyes and threw up his hands in pious joy at the mention of their name, and told

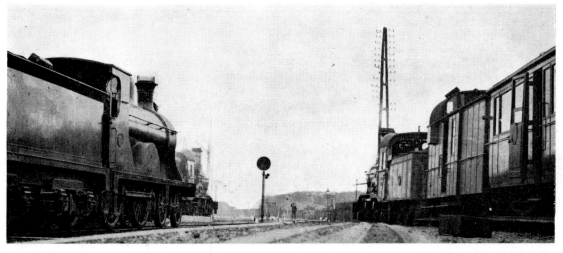

A scene at Ostend : international express trains ready to leave, and 'Dunalastair' engine No 2414 at left centre

An early picture of No 779 'Breadalbane' in dark blue

me with quivering emotion that they were absolute perfection. I don't wonder at it after seeing some of the things they call locomotives over there, for they beat the carriages, many of them, in ugliness. It was a pleasure to see the dignified Scotch giant steaming at his safety valve complacently. . . .'

How long they remained dark blue I cannot say. The later 4—4—0s that were developed from them were painted in the bright green that later became a Belgian standard. It is rather ironical to reflect that the Belgians seem to have had more regard for the historical significance of the 'Dunalastair' than we had—at any rate at the time when their active service was ending. While all the Scottish examples have been scrapped one of the Belgians is preserved.

Reverting now to the Caledonian itself, the fifteen engines of the 'Dunalastair II' class were originally allocated as follows:

766, 767, 768, 769:	Polmadie
770, 771, 772, 773:	Carlisle
774, 775, 776, 777:	Aberdeen
778, 779, 780 :	Perth

It has not been possible to trace the individual drivers who had them at Polmadie and Carlisle, except that Ranochan had No 766 for a time until he changed to No 900 of the 'Dunalastair III' class; but at Perth and Aberdeen the regular men were:

No 775 at Perth, just before grouping. Note 'pop' safety valves

Engine No 778 at Perth, in early days of 'light blue'

Aberdeen:
774 Sam Cuthbert
775 Jock Grassick
776 Harry Mitchell
777 Jim Dailly

Perth:
778 J. McLaren
779 Sandy Brown
780 Will Hamilton

The allocation of engines, no less than the selection of the enginemen, was a highly personal business on the Caledonian Railway. It began in the days of Dugald Drummond. That great man held the view that the driving of express locomotives was such an important job on the railway that the men needed *selection*: not every man who was a

No 780 on Aberdeen express passing Luncarty

53

The second of the 'Dunalastair II', No 767, at Kingmoor. Note detail of the semaphore headcode support

The pioneer engine No 766 'Dunalastair 2nd' on up West Coast express passing Rockcliffe

careful and fully experienced engineman had necessarily the right temperament to drive a fast express, and Drummond travelled extensively on the footplate noting the working of very many drivers, and himself selecting those whom he thought suitable for eventual promotion. It was this policy that had brought such outstanding men as Archie Crooks, Soutar, and Tom Robinson to the fore in time for the Race of 1895, when their temperament for the big occasion was revealed in such strong contrast to that of their rivals on the Great Northern, for example, who had to be tempted by extra pay to run a little harder than usual.

McIntosh, who was above all a 'running' man, continued the practice throughout his chieftainship, and despite war conditions it continued under Pickersgill. On his appointment, in 1895, McIntosh chose for his personal assistant Tom McDonald, who had been locomotive foreman at Polmadie. One of his principal duties was the selection of drivers for express passenger work. The Caledonian Railway despite its growth, and the great increase in its traffic, was not too big for this personal aspect of locomotive manning to be given anything but a very high priority and McDonald, as Drummond had done in earlier days, travelled all over the system as a 'talent scout'. There is no doubt that some splendid men were brought to the fore under this system, at a time when there was intense pride in the job, and suitability, rather than seniority, was the necessary qualification for promotion among the footplate men. Those were the days when an express driver, intensely proud of *his* engine, would give the cleaners a shilling each out of his own pocket to have the buffers polished!

At this stage I am concerned only with the 'Dunalastair II' class in their original condition. Four of them, 766, 767, 771 and 772, were among the earlier Caledonian engines to be superheated. They all had their regular drivers, and they could do some pretty amazing work.

Aberdeen express leaving Perth, passing the ticket platform

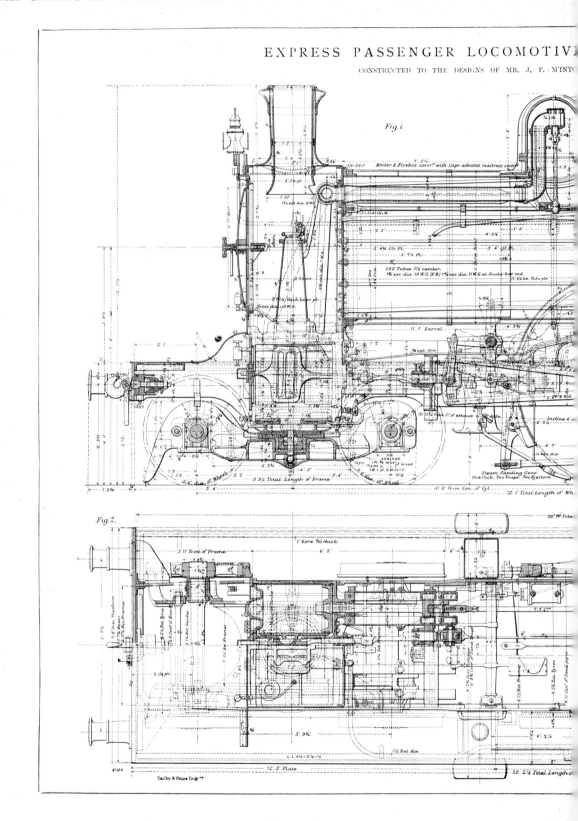

EXPRESS PASSENGER LOCOMOTIVE

CONSTRUCTED TO THE DESIGNS OF MR. J. F. MINTON

THE BELGIAN STATE RAILWAYS.

S. NEILSON, REID, AND CO., ENGINEERS, GLASGOW.

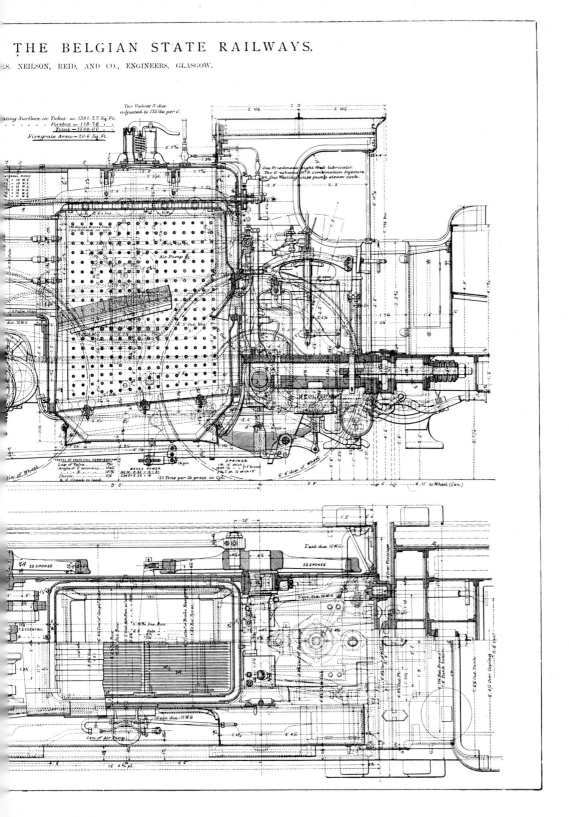

CHAPTER 5

THE 'DUNALASTAIR III' AND 'IV' CLASSES

THE *Glasgow Herald* of 10 December 1899 contained the following news paragraph:

'Mr. John F. McIntosh, Locomotive Superintendent of the Caledonian Railway Company, has just turned out from the St. Rollox Works a number of new engines to which considerable attention is being given from the fact that the far-famed "Dunalastair" class has been put in the shade by their successors the "Breadalbanes" (a class adopted by the Belgian Government with much success for their fast Royal Mail expresses) and that these latter are in turn eclipsed by the new "900" class which are intended by the Directors to cope single handed with the increasing loads of the West Coast expresses over the heavy gradients of the main line.'

After a brief mention of the basic dimensions this news paragraph concluded: 'The special fittings include McIntosh's patent gauge glass protectors; steam saving devices; steam train heating; and the Westinghouse brake. Other special arrangements include the concealment of all pipes, brake rods etc, so as to make the locomotive look as symmetrical as possible.'

At that period in locomotive history much store was still being set upon a neat and handsome exterior. *Engineering,* in an article dated 18 May 1900, emphasises this point strongly:

'Lately there has been an almost universal movement on our railways towards greater tractive power to meet the increasing demands of traffic superintendents and to obviate the makeshifts of a pilot over heavy banks, if not all the way between termini; and we regret to admit that in this long-delayed and now welcome movement the graceful proportions which have nearly always distinguished the British locomotive from those of other countries, have not in all cases been maintained. The handsome appearance of the latest "Dunalastair", however, quite recently put upon the Aberdeen run, leaves nothing to be desired.'

It is always dangerous to express a personal opinion where locomotive aesthetics are concerned, but in its extreme simplicity and perfection of line, I regard the 'Dunalastair III' as one of the most beautiful locomotive classes ever built. It is interesting to see that in contemporary literature the new engines were immediately placed in the 'Dunalastair' family, although no engine of this class ever bore the name. Among Caledonian locomotive men they were known as the '900' class. The first to come out was actually No 902, on 4 December 1899, followed by 900 on the 13th and 901 on the 21st. These three engines completed Works Order Y57; the remaining thirteen engines of the class, Nos 887 to 899, built to Works Order Y62 appeared at intervals between April and July 1900. They represented a notable step forward from the 'Breadalbanes', particularly in respect of the larger firebox. The boiler barrel was exactly the same, though pitched 3 in higher, and the pressure was raised to 180 lb. For ready reference at this stage the respective proportions of the first three 'Dunalastair' classes are tabulated herewith:

'DUNALASTAIR' LOCOMOTIVES

Class		I	II	III
Cylinders diameter	in	$18\frac{1}{4}$	19	19
stroke	in	26	26	26
Boiler:				
Height of centre line above rail level	ft in	7—9	7—9	8—0
Distance between tube plates	ft in	10—7	11—$4\frac{1}{2}$	11—$4\frac{1}{2}$
Mean outside diameter of barrel	ft in	4—$9\frac{1}{4}$	4—$9\frac{1}{4}$	4—$9\frac{1}{4}$
Number of tubes		265	265	269
Outside diameter	in	$1\frac{3}{4}$	$1\frac{3}{4}$	$1\frac{3}{4}$
Total heating surface	sq ft	1403·23	1500·0	1540
Grate area	sq ft	20·63	20·63	23
Working pressure	psi	160	175	180

The first of the 'Dunalastair III' class, No 902, in dark blue livery

It was the use of combination injectors that enabled almost all the external piping to be dispensed with, but a notable difference in working from the earlier engines was the introduction of a steam reverser; which was in fact a combination of a hand lever and steam reversing gear. In reversing the engine the hand lever catch was lifted clear of the notches, steam turned on, and the lever moved forward or back as required. The steam power was there to reduce the actual physical effort in moving the lever. If necessary the lever could be moved without putting on any steam. But as I have already mentioned in connection with actual runs it was the practice of Caledonian drivers to set the reverser in one particular notch, and 'drive on the regulator'. The amount of adjustment of the lever during a run was always at a minimum.

The first three engines went new to Polmadie for working the 'Corridor', and the night sleepers, and were allocated as follows:

900	Driver	Ranochan
901	„	Currie
902	„	Dunn

They at once became great favourites, and for many years it was a saying on the Caledonian 'If in doubt put on a "900" '—even after there were much larger engines available. Of the rest of the class, 887 to 892 were sent new to Perth, and 893 and 898 went to Carlisle. I have not been able to trace the original allocation of No 899, though she may have been at Dalry Road, Edinburgh. The latter shed had otherwise to be content with a single 'Dunalastair' of the first batch, No 731, until No 140 of the fourth series went there in 1904.

The six Perth engines were grouped, in a link of

nine, with the three 'Dunalastair IIs' 778, 779 and 780. The link working of these engines throws a most interesting light upon the duties of engines and men at the turn of the century:

PERTH 'DUNALASTAIR' II and III LINK : 1900

No	Outward	Return
1	5.40 am to Aberdeen	8.20 am Aberdeen-Forfar
		12.15 pm Forfar-Perth
2	5.58 am down Postal to Aberdeen	1.10 pm Aberdeen to Perth
3	9.20 am to Aberdeen	2.0 pm Fish, Aberdeen to Perth
4	8.0 pm up Sleeper to Carlisle	The down 'Tourist' Carlisle to Perth
5	10.5 pm Sleeper to Carlisle	4.22 am Carlisle to Perth
6	8.50 am to Dundee	12.20 pm Dundee via Perth to Symington Return with stock train
7	4.8 pm Fish, to Carlisle	8.30 am stock train Carlisle to Perth
8	11.36 am to Aberdeen	
		5.30 pm Fish, Aberdeen
9	3.19 pm to Aberdeen	8.0 pm Aberdeen to Perth

It will be seen from this that the workings included a mixture of relatively short mileage jobs, Perth to Aberdeen and back 148 miles, and the marathon Carlisle 'single-homes', such as Nos 4 and 5, involving round trips of 300 miles. On No 7 turn the men had a rest intermediately, and this duty alternated with Kingmoor shed. Similarly the two night 'sleeper' jobs were worked on alternate days with

Engine No 889, 'Dunalastair III' class, in Carlisle Citadel station

Kingmoor. Some of the Aberdeen jobs, such as No 2, involved long waits between turns; but I must add that all these workings were long before the introduction of the eight-hour day.

Not many detailed timings of the 'Dunalastair III' class in their early days have been passed down to us today. In September 1902 the 10 am from Glasgow to Carlisle was worked by No 896, with a gross load of 325 tons behind the tender. A 7 ft Connor 2—4—0 was pilot to Carstairs, after which somewhat disappointing work was done to Carlisle, taking 83¼ min for the 73¼-mile run, instead of 81 min allowed. Granted that the schedule was laid out on a pass-to-stop basis; but a time of nothing more enterprising than 50 min 13 sec from Beattock summit to Carlisle was hardly typical of the Caledonian of those days. When Edward Little was on the train almost exactly a year later the work was altogether more interesting, with a load of 380 tons—eleven 8-wheelers and two 12-wheeled dining cars. The pilot, a rebuilt Drummond 4—4—0 No 63, was taken through to Beattock summit.

In the early stages there were slight signal checks at Rutherglen and Cambuslang, and then a 'stop and examine' call led to a dead stop at Uddingston. As a result the train was 7 min late leaving Motherwell. It was good work, even with two engines, to recover 4 min of this by the time the train was away from Beattock summit, where the train was standing for the incredibly short time of 34 sec! The 49·7 miles to Carlisle were then covered in 49 min 53 sec start to stop. There was some good speed between Beattock station and Lockerbie—13·9 miles covered in 13 min 5 sec, and although speed fell off considerably on the short adverse stretches beyond Lockerbie and Kirtlebridge respectively there was a maximum of 75 mph near Gretna. Carlisle was reached in 132 min 50 sec from Glasgow, 2¾ min late. To add a little contemporary background to this journey I can add that the North Western had nothing more modern than two 6 ft 6 in 2—4—0 'Jumbos' to take the 380-ton train on to Crewe, while from the latter place to Rugby an even more antiquated pair of engines was provided, for the up day 'Scotsman': two 'Lady of the Lake' class 2—2—2s, Nos 827 *Victoria* and 279 *Stephenson*, in the year of grace 1903!

On a down journey with the corresponding 10 am from Euston, Edward Little noted quite a good run with engine No 894 and a load of 295 tons gross behind the tender. The train was then nominally non-stop from Carlisle to Glasgow, with 133 min allowed for the 102·3-mile run; but this allowance included a somewhat generous 4 min for locomotive

A 'Dunalastair III' on up West Coast express approaching Beattock summit : engine No 900

purposes at Beattock, and for conditional stops to set down at Symington and Motherwell. After a characteristically rapid start out of Carlisle, passing Rockcliffe, 4·1 miles in 7¼ min, a time of 46 min 26 sec was made to Beattock. The stop there was cut to 1 min 58 sec and with an 0—4—4 tank engine in rear the ten miles to summit were climbed in 18 min 28 sec—a total of 66 min 52 sec from Carlisle. Symington conditional stop was called, with an arrival in 84 min 1 sec from Carlisle, but the Motherwell stop was omitted, and Glasgow Central was reached in 130 min 50 sec from Carlisle, or 126 min 57 sec running time.

Rous-Marten has set on record two runs on the 10.15 am from Edinburgh on which some considerably livelier work was done, both with the same driver, Stavert, though with different engines. The two runs, as between Strawfrank Junction and Carlisle, are tabulated herewith:

These were both very fine performances. The average speeds of 49·1 and 50 mph between Symington and Beattock summit indicate first-class uphill work, with a load of 305 tons, while the speeds south of Beattock station, particularly on the second run, are equally indicative of the freedom with which these engines could run. Stavert was

CALEDONIAN RAILWAY
STRAWFRANK JUNCTION—CARLISLE

Engine No		899		896	
Load tons full		305		305	
Dist		Time m s	Av speed mph	Time m s	Av speed mph
0·0	Strawfrank Junction	0 00	—	0 00	—
6·6	SYMINGTON	10 26	37·3	9 54	40·0
23·8	*Summit*	31 29	49·1	30 32	50·0
33·8	BEATTOCK	41 52	57·7	40 10	62·3
47·7	Lockerbie	54 11	67·7	51 59	70·6
60·5	Kirkpatrick	66 41	61·3	63 46	65·7
64·9	Gretna	70 16	73·6	67 25	72·3
67·4	Floriston	72 13	76·8	68 35	69·3
69·4	Rockcliffe	73 58	68·6	71 30	62·7
73·5	CARLISLE	78 04		75 54	

A head-end view of No 901, showing details of construction, and an interesting contemporary signal

certainly an expert driver, and in all probability he was putting on a special show for Rous-Marten; but even with these reservations the two runs mark the 'Dunalastair IIIs' as exceedingly good engines.

In May 1902, Lord Monkswell rode engine No 902 on the down 'Corridor' from Carlisle to Glasgow, with a load of 320 tons gross behind the tender, and experienced a very fine run. He records that the lever was put into the seventh notch (out of 20 from full forward to full reverse) soon after starting, and use of full regulator provided a very rapid start, passing Rockcliffe 4·1 miles in 6 min 36 sec. Thereafter the regulator opening varied between one-half and two-thirds full onwards to Beattock. A maximum of 62 mph was attained at the Solway Firth; the long 1 in 200 to Kirkpatrick was taken at around 50 mph, and there was a maximum of 72 mph after Lockerbie. So Beattock, 39·7 miles, was reached in 44 min 43 sec—quite up to the standard of work regularly put up by *Cardean* in later years on this train.

Lord Monkswell comments: 'The engine had

run remarkably smoothly and was nowhere in the slightest difficulty. The fire appeared to be rather thin—well below the firehole door behind where all the fresh fuel was put on. The firing was more or less continuous, but all done in the most leisurely way, the fireman raising the deflector plate with his right hand just enough to get in the shovel with his left, and dropping the coal under the firehole.

'At Beattock we stopped for an engine behind and, after a minute and a quarter delay, started up the bank, with two fountains of sparks shooting out of the chimneys of the engines into the darkness of the night. The ten miles to the summit took $18\frac{1}{2}$ minutes, and then, dropping the bank engine, we had a fairly good run downhill to Strawfrank Junction. From passing Elvanfoot to the stop at Strawfrank $20\frac{1}{2}$ miles took 19 min. 8 sec. and the highest speed (Crawford to Lamington 7m. 76ch. in 6 min. 44 sec.) was 70 m.p.h. On this downhill run the engine did not run so steadily as when she had been working harder on the level and uphill, and in one or two places where the permanent way was out of order, she rocked very badly. The 33¼ miles from Beattock to Strawfrank start to stop, took 40 min. 47 sec.'

One can add that 18½ min, start to pass, from Beattock station to the summit was an exceedingly fine time for a 'Dunalastair III' and an 0—4—4 tank with a 320-ton train. No wonder there were two fountains of sparks! The overall time from Carlisle to Strawfrank Junction was 86 min 45 sec. After detaching the Edinburgh portion they got a bad road, and after being stopped dead by signals several times arrived in Glasgow 10 min late. Lord Monkswell records in his journal that he was up early next morning to catch the 4.20 am from Buchanan Street, and join the down 'Postal' at Stirling. A 'Dunalastair III', No 895 brought in the train from the south, but with a very light load and several checks they got a poor run to Perth. Then, with load increased by one coach to a total of 85 tons behind the tender a 'Dunalastair II' came on, No 780. Lord Monkswell adds: 'The driver was a very young man. He looked about 30 and seemed intelligent . . .'—clearly one of Tom McDonald's choices. They started most vigorously, and despite a sharp signal check to 15 mph at Woodside covered the 32½ miles to Forfar in 32 min 25 sec. Speed on the level was 75 to 77 mph. After that no particular effort was needed, and Aberdeen was reached in 93 min 44 sec.

The completion of the 'Dunalastair III' class with engine No 894, turned out from St Rollox in June 1900, marked the end of 4—4—0 locomotive building on the Caledonian Railway for nearly four years. By that time there was a stud of forty-six splendid engines, which together with the rebuilt Drummonds was coping very satisfactorily with the passenger work of the line. The drawing office was nevertheless very active, and in the years 1901-3 several new designs made their appearance, including the huge 4—6—0s Nos 49 and 50, designed for the heaviest expresses between Glasgow and Carlisle. These two engines were to a large extent experimental, and 4—4—0 building was resumed in 1904, with the introduction of the 'Dunalastair IV' series, more generally known on the line as the '140' class. The first order 'Y72' was for five engines, completed in May and June 1904, and this was followed by another six on order 'Y76' turned out between November 1905 and January 1906.

The introduction of these engines led Charles Rous-Marten into the writing of one of the most extraordinary essays of his career. At the time G. J. Churchward, on the Great Western, was causing a considerable stir in railway circles by his use of tapered boiler barrels. He was being widely criticised for spoiling the traditional handsome appearance of British locomotives. But to return to the Caledonian, somehow or other Rous-Marten seems to have got the idea that the boiler barrels of the 'Dunalastair IV' class were tapered. In an article contributed to *The Engineer* in December 1905 he wrote: 'In outward aspect the boilers of these newer engines are perfect cylinders, without any sign of coning or taper; in reality, however, they are of the wagon-top order, like those introduced on the Great Western, by Mr. Churchward, that is to say, ex-

A 'Dunalastair IV' No 146 on up stopping train at Gretna Junction

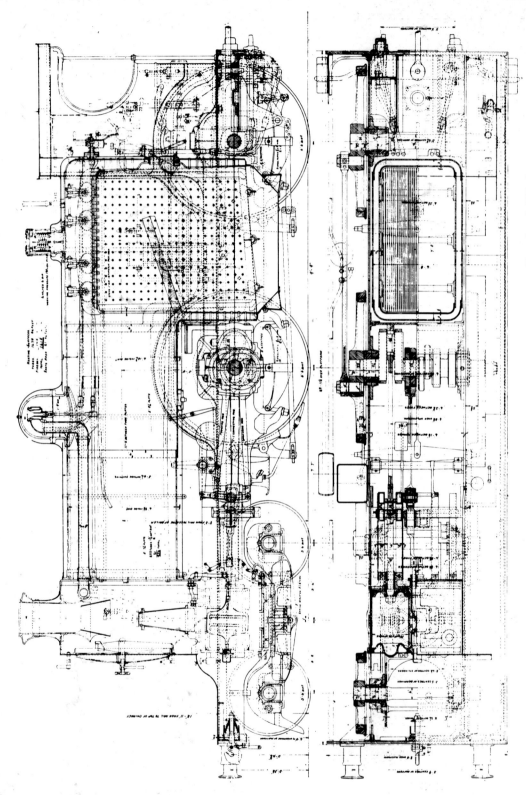

Reproduction of the official general arrangement of the non-superheater 'Dunalastair IV' class

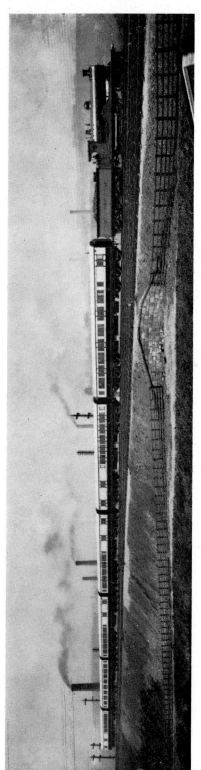

The Grampian 'Corridor' express posed near St Rollox, with 'Dunalastair IV' engine No 144

Glasgow portion of 10 am ex-Euston passing Kingmoor,
hauled by 'Dunalastair III' No 899

Down West Coast express approaching Beattock summit
hauled by 'Dunalastair III' No 897

E

panding outwardly towards the firebox, so that the diameter at the point where the firebox is met is slightly in excess of that at the smokebox end, or at mid-way in the boiler length.'

After a somewhat lengthy dissertation on what the technical term for a tapered boiler should be, Rous-Marten went on to emphasise that Churchward had taken the purely non-aesthetic view so far as the appearance of the engines were concerned, and had said to Rous-Marten: 'People may say that these boilers are ugly; but they do their work, and that is what I want.' It was then that Rous-Marten went on to make the most extraordinary statement. Referring to Churchward's dictum, he went on: 'This, of course, is perfectly sound reasoning; nevertheless Mr. McIntosh felt reluctant that his engines should lose the external symmetry for which they had long been admired, and so he determined, while adopting the new shape of boiler, to retain the old symmetrical form by carrying forward the lagging and sheeting in a straight line from smokebox to firebox, thus leaving the exterior of the boiler a perfect cylinder as before.'

Whether McIntosh ever considered the use of the truly tapered boiler, either of the short-cone, or of the full-cone type as used on the Great Western, one cannot now say. He may have done,

and confided his intentions to Rous-Marten; but the drawing of the first five of the 'Dunalastair IV' class, dated 28 March 1904, shows no more 'taper' than the difference in diameter of the forward and after rings, due to the thickness of the plates. The forward ring had an inside diameter of 4 ft 9½ in, and with ⅝ in thick plates the diameter of the after ring was 4 ft 10¾ in. The barrel was thus no more than slightly larger than that of the first three 'Dunalastair' classes, though there was a slight rearrangement of the tubes, to provide 255 with an outside diameter of 1¾ in and 21 with an outside diameter of 2 in. This gave a tube heating surface of 1,470 sq ft as against 1,402 sq ft in the 'Dunalastair III', and the firebox heating surface was increased to 145 sq ft, against 138, though the grate area was *reduced* from 23 to 21 sq ft. The boiler barrel had its centre line pitched 3 in higher than in the third series, thus increasing the already massive, though exceedingly handsome, appearance of the engines.

So far as taper barrels were concerned, at the time Rous-Marten wrote his article in *The Engineer* only the first five of the 'Dunalastair IVs' were at work; but a drawing associated with a later batch of these engines, order Y85, and covering the five engines Nos 923 to 927 turned out between Decem-

The 10 am express Glasgow to Euston, on the last stage to Beattock summit with 'Dunalastair IV' engine No 925. Note the driver giving attention to a bogie axle-box tending to heat!

One of the first batch of 'Dunalastair IV' class 4—4—0s, No 142

ber 1907 and February 1908, shows an enlarged boiler barrel, though no more tapered than the original one of 1904. On the 923-927 batch the forward ring was 4 ft 10¾ in diameter and the after one 5 ft diameter. The heating surfaces remained the same. The bogie tender was even larger than those attached to the 'Dunalastair III' class, providing for 4,300 gallons of water and 4½ tons of coal. The engine weight in working order was 56½ tons, while the tender weighed 50¾ tons—a heavy price to pay, in non-productive haulage, for not having water troughs on the line. Even so the ultimate in 4—4—0 tender size had not yet been reached on the Caledonian Railway. The 'Dunalastair IV' class were turned out in the lighter blue that later became so well known as 'Caley blue', as distinct from the Prussian blue of earlier days.

When new, engines 140 and 141 were on the Edinburgh trains; but 141 was transferred early to Aberdeen for the through workings to Carlisle. No 144 went new to Perth, and 142 and 143 were at Kingmoor. In many ways these tremendously hard working engines were the Caledonian equiva-

lent of the North Western 'Precursors', and they had not long been in service before the pioneer engine had achieved a performance that ranks among the classics of Scottish railway history. Rous-Marten has described how he found engine No 140 heading an enormous train 'extending from the buffer stops at Princes Street station to a van's length outside of the platform end'. The gross load behind the tender was estimated at 404 tons, and a 7 ft rebuilt Connor 2—4—0 was attached as pilot to Cobbinshaw. This initial distance of 18.4 miles was covered in 28 min 57 sec start to stop, and No 140, with Driver Stavert in charge, was left to cover the remaining 82.2 miles to Carlisle unassisted. The overall tendency of the road is of course downhill; but intermediately there was the ascent of 23.5 miles from Strawfrank Junction to Beattock summit, which was no light task for a non-superheater 4—4—0 engine hauling 404 tons.

Tantalisingly, Rous-Marten gives no details of the point-to-point times made on the ascent of the Clyde valley—only the speeds; and here I quote in full from an article he wrote in *The Engineer* for

Down West Coast express passing Kingmoor yards, hauled by 'Dunalastair IV' 4—4—0 No 141

8 December 1905: 'After slowing through Strawfrank Junction, the speed steadily increased up the subsequent two miles, rising at 1 in 150, until a rate of 42·9 miles an hour was reached, the same point being attained up the short length at 1 in 100 approaching Symington. South of that station, and before Lamington, comes one of the short "breathing places", two miles of easy descent, where our speed soon rose to 60 miles an hour. Up the 10 miles of unbroken ascent, chiefly at 1 in 150, 1 in 200, and 1 in 300 between Lamington and Elvanfoot, the speed never fell below 43 miles an hour, and the average was 46·5. But the final two miles of 1 in 100 to the Beattock summit constituted the real crux of the whole journey. Here the speed

at first dropped steadily, as was certain to be the case with so vast a load on such a grade. In the end it fell to exactly 36 miles an hour, but at this point it kept steadily, quarter-mile after quarter-mile, until the summit was reached, each quarter-mile being covered in exactly 25 seconds, as tested by two chronographs, whose respective starting and stopping buttons were pressed simultaneously as each quarter-mile post was passed. The engine never showed the least sign of flagging or slipping, and was "going strong" as ever when the summit was breasted.'

That sustained 36 mph on a gradient of 1 in 100, with a load of 404 tons, takes some believing. Furthermore, Rous-Marten does not say how many quarter-miles were thus covered. One could infer from his writing that there were quite a few. But if he happened to be one-fifth of a second out on two of them, and the last three quarter-miles took 24 4/5, 25, and 25 1/5 sec, giving speeds of 36·3, 36, and 35·7 mph, the horsepower involved would have been considerably less. Taking Rous-Marten's words exactly as they are, a sustained 36 mph would have involved an equivalent drawbar horsepower of at least 1,300. It could easily have been more, because the rolling-stock in use at that time most likely had a higher rolling resistance than modern corridor stock. At that speed, an equivalent drawbar horsepower of 1,300 would have represented a drawbar pull of 6 tons. This is 73 per cent of the nominal tractive effort of the engine—certainly a very high figure, but by no means impossible. I have personally seen a Great Northern large-boilered 'Atlantic' produce just over 60 per cent of her nominal tractive effort for a few thrilling

Up express on the last stage of the climb to Beattock summit, hauled by engine No 146 with smokebox very lavishly adorned

minutes, and *Cardean* did slightly better than this in some of her 'interchange' running with the LNWR in 1909. If Stavert threw in all he had, for Rous-Marten's benefit, on that final ascent to Beattock summit, I can believe he was very near a sustained minimum speed of 36 mph.

Minutiae apart, it was a magnificent performance, and it was followed by some fast running south of Beattock. Here again, while it is clear Rous-Marten was logging in close detail, he published only the outline of the run. Speed was 76½ mph at the crossing of the Annan, near Wamphray; it fell gradually off to 50 mph at Castlemilk sidings, and reached 80½ mph on the final descent from Kirkpatrick to Gretna. Overall, the 82.2 miles from Cobbinshaw summit to Carlisle were covered in 87 min 21 sec start to stop, and the overall time from Edinburgh, 100·6 miles, was 117 min 50 sec.

Rous-Marten also recorded a most spectacular performance with the corresponding down train. At the time this was a purely London-Edinburgh express, including no more reinforcement than a through carriage from Birmingham, and it preceded the Glasgow section of the 10 am from Euston after division at Crewe. On this occasion the departure from Carlisle was very late. This was fortunate, because the working time allowed was then as much as 134 min non-stop to Princes Street, and with a load of only 170 tons behind the tender the effort required would have been negligible. The engine this time was No 141, driven by Watt. Despite bad weather, and slippery rails, the start was tremendous. A speed of 75 mph was attained at the Solway Firth; there was nothing less than 60 mph on either of the long 1 in 200 ascents that follow, and Lockerbie, 25·8 miles, was passed in 24 min 55 sec, at 77½ mph. The next 13·9 miles on to Beattock were taken flying in 12 min 24 sec—67·2 mph average—and in such style there was every chance of clearing Beattock summit in about 50 min from the start.

Then unfortunately the train was stopped dead by signal at Auchencastle box, and held for 2 min 43 sec. The restart had to be made right on the 1 in 75 gradient, in drizzling rain, but speed was quickly worked up to 36 mph. There was some slipping on the curves near Greskine box, causing a drop to 33 mph, but thereafter the 36 mph was regained and sustained then unbrokenly to Beattock summit. In such circumstances it was excellent work to climb the complete ten miles of the bank in 19 min 38 sec with a dead stop of 2 min 43 sec intermediately. The equivalent drawbar horsepower involved in this case was 900. Although not such a spectacular effort as that of No 140 on the southbound train this was nevertheless exceedingly fine work, involving a drawbar pull of almost 50 per cent of the nominal tractive effort of the engine. After passing Beattock summit in 56 min 57 sec from Carlisle, delay included, the remaining 50·9 miles to Edinburgh took 53¼ min, completing the run in 110 min 12 sec from Carlisle. Rous-Marten gives no details of the ascent to Cobbinshaw, nor of the downhill speeds in Upper Clydesdale. One can only infer that the latter were no more than moderate, as the maximum speed of the whole journey occurred near Lockerbie.

While these were undoubtedly special efforts, put on for Rous-Marten's benefit, there is no doubt that the 'Dunalastair IV' class were very capable machines. They certainly used a lot of coal in the process, about which there is a good story to be told later. But now there is one more run of 1905 to be mentioned. The smart booking of 32 min start to stop for the up 'Grampian', from Forfar to Perth (32·5 miles), was not publicly booked, presumably due to the general uneasiness that prevailed just then about high-speed running. But the 'Dunalastair IVs' in their early days made light of the schedule. The regular Perth driver on No 144 was the celebrated 'Cuddy' Mitchell, and one day when Rous-Marten was a passenger he worked a 260 ton load from Forfar to Perth in 31 min 1 sec start to stop, including a maximum speed of 83½ mph. The 'Dunalastair IVs' could certainly 'fly' in their early days, and they were reputed to ride very steadily. Not all observers of the period were accorded the same privileges as Rous-Marten. The late E. C. Poultney once told me how he approached McIntosh for a footplate pass on the up 'Grampian' to test this very run. But old 'J.F.M.' laughed his request aside, with the remark: 'Och, ye'd fall off!'

CHAPTER 6

INTRODUCTION OF SUPERHEATING

AFTER the completion of the 923-927 series of 'Dunalastair IV' engines in 1907 there was a pause in 4—4—0 building at St Rollox; but in 1910 an order, Y92, was placed for a further four engines of the class, Nos 136-139, and the first three were turned out in June-July of that year. At that time, however, intense interest was being taken in the possibilities of superheating. At Crewe, Bowen-Cooke was building the first LNWR engine to be so equipped, and so McIntosh obtained authority to re-design the last engine of order Y92 to be superheater equipped. This engine, No 139, completed at St Rollox in July 1910, was the first superheater engine to run in Scotland. The process of re-design was considerable. The cylinder diameter was increased to 20 in; the frames were strengthened, an extended smokebox fitted, and the boiler pressure lowered to 165 psi. Despite this latter, the nominal tractive effort was increased from 18,411 lb in the '140' class to 18,700 lb. McIntosh clearly looked to superheating as a means of reducing boiler maintenance charges by reduction of the working pressure.

On engine No 139 the very simple arrangement of slide valves between the cylinders, worked by direct Stephenson's link motion, which had been traditional on the Caledonian since the days of Dugald Drummond, was at last abandoned, and in conjunction with the large cylinders, 20 in diameter, piston valves 8 in diameter were mounted above the cylinders and actuated by rocking levers. Although there was space between the cylinders, vacant through the removal of valves, the distance between the cylinder centre lines remained the same as in the 'Dunalastair IV' class, 2 ft 4½ in. It was not possible to reduce this dimension because of the space needed on the driving axle, between the crank webs, to get in the four eccentrics of the Stephenson link motion. On the 'Dunalastair IV' non-super-heater engines there was an aperture in the frame to permit the cylinders to be accommodated, trans-verse width-wise, and this of course was greater on No 139, with 20 in instead of 19 in cylinders. Like her LNWR counterpart, No 2663 *George the Fifth*, No 139 had a Schmidt type superheater, with that engineer's patent piston rings, and trick-ported valves. Four further engines of this class were built in April and May 1911 to order Y97, Nos 132-5.

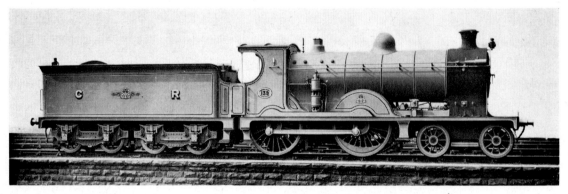

The first superheater engine in Scotland : engine No 139 of the 'Dunalastair IV' class, built 1910

The Grampian 'Corridor' express leaving Stirling, hauled by
'Dunalastair IV' engine No 140

In view of their contemporary appearance, and of the strong links existing between the Caledonian and London & North Western Railways it is interesting to compare the basic dimensions of these two pioneer superheater engines, especially since both classes underwent slight enlargements afterwards. On the Crewe engine the cylinders were increased from 20 to $20\frac{1}{2}$ in diameter; on the St Rollox engine the cylinders were increased from 20 to $20\frac{1}{4}$ in diameter, and the working pressure from 165 to 170 psi.

The later engines of the McIntosh superheated class were numbered in order of construction, 117 to 122, 43 to 48, 39 to 42 and 123; those numbered from 121 onwards differed in having Robinson superheaters with a slightly reduced amount of heating surface, namely 295 instead of 330 sq ft.

Engine No 139 went new to Perth, and was allocated to Driver J. Mitchell, 'Cuddy', whose fireman was G. Walker. On the Carlisle run they immediately began to show a remarkable saving in coal over the non-superheater '140' class. Comparative trials were carried out between this engine and No 138, and the results were communicated by McIntosh himself to the Rev W. J. Scott. The trials

WEST COAST 4—4—0 SUPERHEATER ENGINES JULY 1910

Railway			LNWR	Caledonian
Engine No			2663	139
Cylinders:	diameter	in	20	20
	stroke	in	26	26
Coupled wheel dia	ft in		6—9	6—6
Total evap heating surface		sq ft	1546·7	1365
Superheater		sq ft	302·5	330
Combined total		sq ft	1849·2	1695
Grate area		sq ft	22·4	21
Working pressure		psi	175	165
Nominal tractive effort at 85% BP			19,100	18,700

CALEDONIAN RAILWAY : COAL TRIALS, 1910

Engine No	138	139
Type	Saturated	Superheated
Tender ⎰ coal	$4\frac{1}{2}$ tons	6 tons
Capacity ⎱ water	4,300 gal	4,600 gal
Total weight of engine and tender in working order, tons	$112\frac{1}{2}$	115
Average trailing load tons:		
southbound	265	220
northbound	220	235
Total coal, for 3 retn trips lb	42,292	33,520
Coal, lb per train mile	47·5	37·2
Coal, per gross ton mile	0·138	0·106
Evaporation, total water gal	27,495	22,138

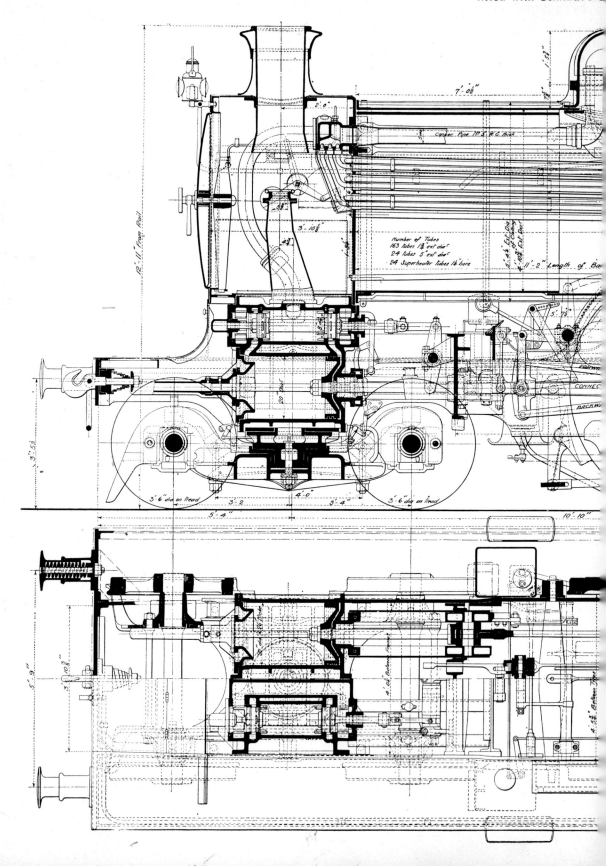

Number of Tubes:
163 tubes 1¾" ext dia!
24 tubes 5" ext dia!
24 Superheater tubes 1¼ bore

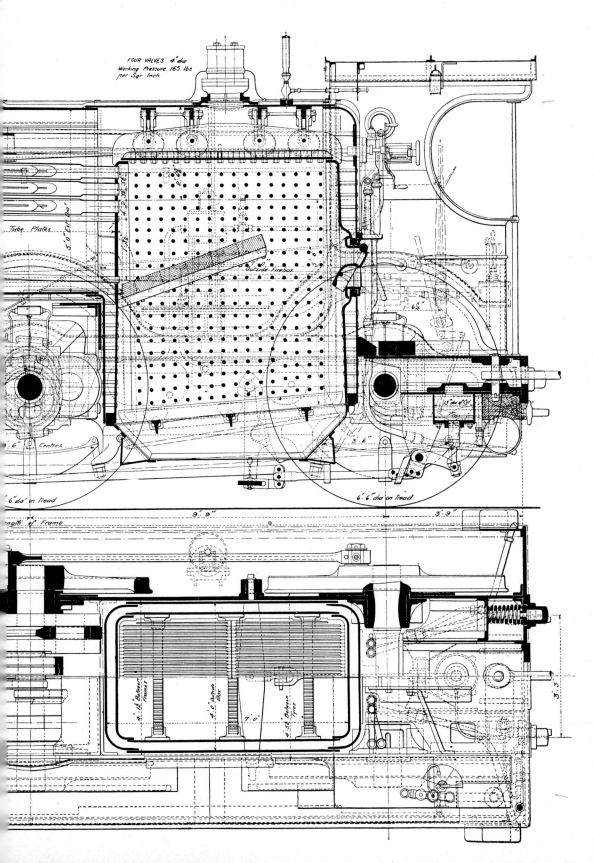

FOUR VALVES 4″ dia
Working Pressure 165 lbs
per Sqr Inch

A broadside of a superheated 'Dunalastair IV' No 120, at St Rollox, showing the handsome proportions of engine and tender

were extended over three return trips from Perth to Carlisle and back, single home, on the 9 pm up sleeper, and back with the down 'Tourist', then leaving Carlisle at 2.20 am. The results were as shown on the previous page.

These results showed a saving of 23 per cent in coal and 25 per cent in water. No assistance was taken on any of the banks, and for a road like that between Perth and Carlisle, with Gleneagles and Beattock summits to surmount, the overall consumption of 37 lb per mile by No 139 must be considered very good. In view of the previous comparison in dimensions between this first Caledonian superheater engine and the LNWR 'George the Fifth' class, when it comes to loads the great difference between the size of the tenders must be taken into account: Caledonian, 56 tons; LNWR, 37 tons. Thus, No 139 would be hauling roughly 20 tons extra, in a direct comparison between the two engines, and an equivalent load of 255 tons on the

down 'Tourist' was certainly no light proposition.

In addition to the comparative coal trials on the Carlisle road engine No 139 was indicated while working the 'Grampian Corridor Express' between Glasgow and Perth. Records are available of fourteen diagrams, taken mostly on heavy uphill sections on the down journey.

These details are interesting as showing the cut-off percentages corresponding to the different notches, and also that the engine was pulled up to 21 per cent for the faster stretches. The diagrams themselves show excellent characteristics, and by way of explanation of the differences in horsepower between some of them, under apparently similar conditions—diagrams 5 and 6, for example—I may add that the regulator openings were being varied, as well as the lever positions. The load of the train was 205 tons behind the tender, a total weight, including engine and tender, of 320 tons.

During the trials engine No 138 was worked by

Diagram No	Location	Lever notch	Cut-off %	Speed mph	Mean effective pressure psi	Indicated horse-power
1	St Rollox	6th	60	$18\frac{1}{2}$	119	784
2	Milepost 103	5th	52	23	109	900
3	„ $102\frac{1}{4}$	4th	42	27	93	888
4	Robroyston	3rd	32	$32\frac{1}{2}$	77	888
5	Garnkirk	2nd	21	$50\frac{1}{4}$	53	940
6	Glenboig	2nd	21	$51\frac{1}{4}$	43	780
7	Milepost 98	2nd	21	56	45	888
8	„ $121\frac{1}{4}$	3rd	32	42	61	904
9	Dunblane	3rd	32	$30\frac{3}{4}$	77	836
10	Milepost 124	3rd	32	26	74	684
11	„ $124\frac{1}{2}$	3rd	32	$23\frac{1}{4}$	81	654
12	„ 125	3rd	32	$21\frac{1}{2}$	84	636
13	„ $125\frac{1}{2}$	3rd	32	$21\frac{1}{2}$	84	636
14	Kinbuck	3rd	32	26	78	720

Note: the mileposts relate to the mileage from Carlisle *via* Coatbridge

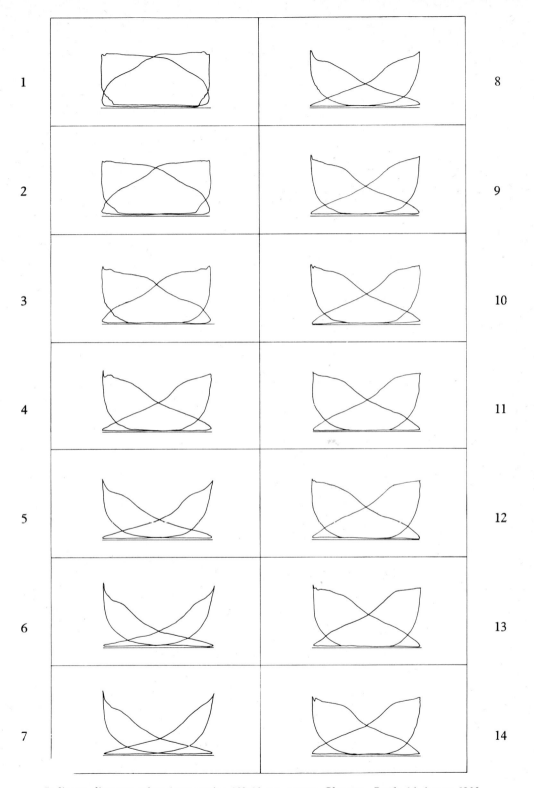

Indicator diagrams taken from engine 139:10 am express Glasgow - Perth:16 August 1910.
For locations etc, see table opposite

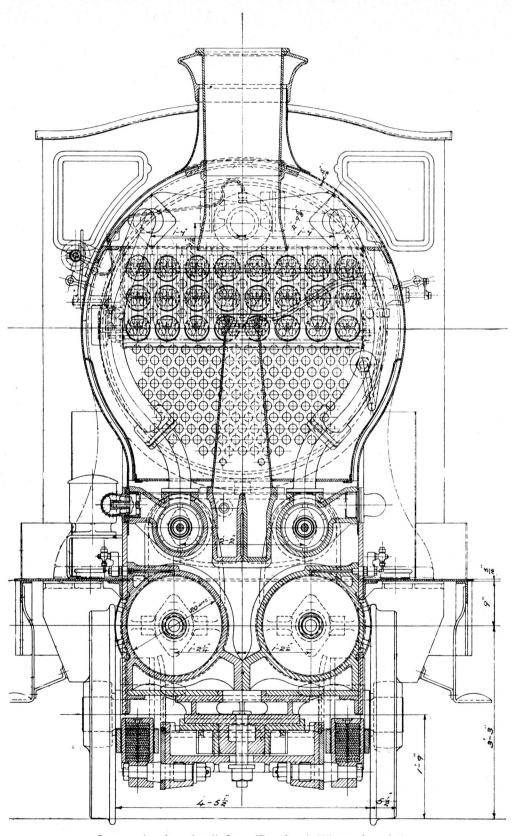

Cross-section through cylinders : 'Dunalastair IV' superheated class

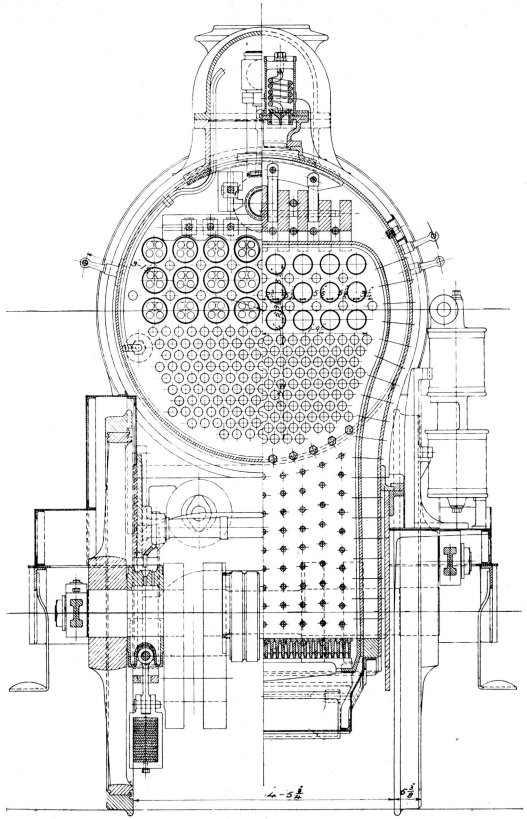

Cross-section at dome : 'Dunalastair IV' superheated class

Aberdeen - Edinburgh express near Stanley Junction hauled by superheater 'Dunalastair IV' No 44

Driver W. Wishart and Fireman Jock McLeish, but the latter went on to No 133 (superheater) when that engine was allocated to Perth, with Driver Peter Thompson. They did splendid work on the Carlisle single-home jobs, and did the night's work on eight to nine boxes of coal—about 4 to 4½ tons. All that was necessary in the turn-round time at Carlisle was to get coal forward. The load put on at Perth was all they needed for the round trip. This would mean less than 35 lb per mile. But McLeish has told how, when 133 went into the shops they got their old friend No 138 again, and on the same work burned 14 to 16 boxes according to the load and prevailing weather. To appreciate the following story to the full it must be understood that 'lum' is the Scots vernacular for chimney. One night Thompson and 'Cuddy' Mitchell changed shifts, and McLeish fired to Mitchell on the non-superheater engine No 138. As usual they needed more coal when they got to Carlisle. McLeish then said: 'I was cleaning the fire, and Cuddy was attending to the coaling. He got box after box put on, and then he shouted to the coalman, "That's enough". That worthy replied, "Back a bit", and as the engine moved he yelled "Stop". Cuddy asked what was up, and the coalman replied, "Take a box down the b—— lum and you'll maybe have enough!"'

The superheated 'Dunalastair IVs' were distributed only between Kingmoor, Perth and Aberdeen sheds. Perth had eight of them, and the other two sheds seven each. It will be appreciated that the bulk of the most important express work of the Caledonian fell to these three sheds. Balornock and Polmadie had a few special turns, as with the 'Corridors' in the latter case; but the 10 am up 'Scotsman' from Glasgow Central to Euston, and the up night sleeper were Kingmoor turns. The original allocations were:

Aberdeen Engine No	Kingmoor Engine No	Perth Engine No
40	47	39
41	48	45
42	121	46
43	122	119
44	123	120
117	134	132
118	135	133
—	—	139

The engines fitted with the Schmidt superheaters, that is 139, 132 to 135, and 117 to 120, had superheater dampers operated by a small steam cylinder on the right-hand side of the smokebox, and controlled by a large brass wheel in the cab. The engines with the Robinson superheaters also had damper gear, but it was controlled by a system of cranks—entirely by hand. There was no servo cylinder to assist. In the use of superheater dampers under the control of the driver the Caledonian was in line with current practice on the LNWR, and if skilfully used this arrangement could be of assistance when starting cold with a heavy train. With the fire not fully burned through pressure might be dropped, and the steaming affected for a long time; but by partially closing the damper the bulk of the flue gases would be driven through the small tubes. There might be a loss of superheat temperature but the pressure would be maintained.

On the Caledonian, as elsewhere, it was found that the non-superheated engines were much smarter in getting away from a cold start; in fact, a saturated 'Dunalastair IV' would beat a superheater, in comparable loading conditions, from Carlisle right out to Beattock station; but the superheater engine would by then be thoroughly warmed up to assert her inherent superiority in climbing the bank itself. It was the same starting southbound from Perth. The Caledonian men when preparing the superheater engines used to try and heat up the brick arch as much as possible before starting, by keeping a thin, clear fire. They only began really to pile on the coal just before starting. In later years the impression grew that the Caledonian engines generally were heavy on coal. This was probably due to the performance of the Pickersgills, and particularly to the poor results obtained with engine No 124 in the trials on the Midland in 1924. But the superheated 'Dunalastair IV' class were really excellent engines. It was nothing unusual for them

to run the down 'Tourist' over the 150 miles from Carlisle to Perth without taking water intermediately, which would mean a consumption of only about 30 gallons a mile, while if the Oban portion was run separately they had no qualms about running the 150 miles non-stop.

Although the down 'Tourist' was not nearly so fast as in the days of the first 'Dunalastairs' it was no light proposition, being allowed 143 min for the $117\frac{3}{4}$ miles from Carlisle to Stirling. Cecil J. Allen had an interesting run on the second portion of this train in the height of the summer season, in 1913, when a load of 400 tons was taken by superheater 4—4—0 No 120, piloted to Beattock summit by a 'Dunalastair III', No 896. The two engines passed Beattock station, 39.7 miles, in 41 min 40 sec, and stopped at the summit in 60 min 5 sec. Then after detaching the pilot, No 120 took the 400 ton train onwards to Stirling in 78 min 25 sec, 68 miles, inclusive of two signal checks, and restrained running on most of the downhill sections other than the Clyde valley between summit and Carstairs. This train was mostly for Oban, and a load of no more than 160 tons remained after Stirling.

In the years just before World War I there were two turns on which the engines and men worked through between Carlisle and Aberdeen, with Kingmoor and Aberdeen men on alternate days. The two turns were:

1. 6.40 am Aberdeen to Carlisle
    2.54 am Down 'Postal', Carlisle to Aberdeen
2. 1.12 pm Carlisle to Aberdeen
    3.40 pm Up 'Postal', Aberdeen to Carlisle

The ill-fated 121 on one of the regular pre-war turns : the 10.5 am Glasgow-Liverpool and Manchester express here seen near Floriston. This engine was damaged beyond repair in the Quintinshill disaster

Engine No 136, 'Dunalastair IV' class, fitted with the Weir feed water heater, in 1920

These workings originated in the days of Dugald Drummond; but they were suspended for a while, to be reinstated with the 'Dunalastair III' engines. As soon as they were available, however, the superheated 'Dunalastair IVs' took them on. They were of course eminently suitable for this work, because of their low coal and water consumption.

Detailed logs of the working of these engines in their early days are scarce. The accompanying details show the running of the down 'Tourist', engine No 132 in the summer of 1913. With a load of 255 tons a stop was made for rear-end assistance up Beattock bank. It was a smart piece of work,

with a start-to-stop of 42 min 23 sec from Carlisle to Beattock, and an average speed of 56·2 mph. No details are available for the subsequent running, though nothing very strenuous would have been demanded after passing summit. Another log, tabulated herewith, shows the work of one of the non-superheated 'Dunalastair IVs' at about the

2.20 am CARLISLE—BEATTOCK
Load : 255 tons gross
Engine : Superheater 4—4—0 No 132

Dist miles				Actual m s	Av speed mph
0·0	CARLISLE	.	.	0 00	—
4·1	Rockcliffe	.	.	6 10	—
6·1	Floriston	.	.	8 05	62·7
8·6	Gretna Junc	.	.	10 23	65·2
13·0	Kirkpatrick	.	.	15 23	52·8
16·7	Kirtlebridge	.	.	19 39	52·1
20·1	Ecclefechan	.	.	23 45	49·8
25·8	LOCKERBIE	.	.	28 51	67·1
28·7	Nethercleugh	.	.	31 24	68·2
31·7	Dinwoodie	.	.	34 06	68·0
34·5	Wamphray	.	.	36 48	62·0
39·7	BEATTOCK	.	.	42 23	

11.26 am SYMINGTON—CARLISLE
Load : 285 tons gross
Engine : Non-superheater 4—4—0 No 137

Dist miles				Actual m s	Speeds mph
0·0	SYMINGTON	.	.	0 00	—
3·7	Lamington	.	.	6 18	—
8·9	Abington	.	.	12 25	51·0
11·6	Crawford	.	.	15 40	49·9
14·3	Elvanfoot	.	.	19 22	43·8
17·2	*Summit*	.	.	23 38	40·8*
27·2	BEATTOCK	.	.	34 52	53·3
32·4	Wamphray	.	.	40 07	59·4
35·2	Dinwoodie	.	.	42 53	60·7
38·2	Nethercleugh	.	.	45 41	64·3
41·1	LOCKERBIE	.	.	49 14	—
5·7	Ecclefechan	.	.	9 10	—
9·1	Kirtlebridge	.	.	12 26	63·0
12·8	Kirkpatrick	.	.	16 05	60·6
17·1	Gretna Junc	.	.	20 19	61·3
19·7	Floriston	.	.	22 45	64·1
21·7	Rockcliffe	.	.	24 50	57·5
25·8	CARLISLE	.	.	30 51	

* Minimum speed at Summit 35.7 mph

same time. The train was 5 min late in leaving Symington, but Carlisle was reached practically on time. The work was not exceptional at any point, but it is reproduced to show contemporary performance of the non-superheated engines. As with previous Caledonian 4—4—0 engines the superheater 'Dunalastair IVs' all had their regular drivers, and their names are given in one of the appendixes. This practice continued well into the war years, and in the case of one of the Kingmoor engines, No 121, engine and crew ended their days together in the Quintinshill disaster.

The success of superheating on the 'Dunalastair IV' class led to the rebuilding of some of the older engines with superheaters. In 1914 three 'Dunalastair IIs' and two 'Dunalastair IIIs' were so treated, as follows:

'Dunalastair II'	No 766 rebuilt	Oct	1914
"	" 771 "	March	1914
"	" 772 "	July	1914
'Dunalastair III'	" 901 "	March	1914
"	" 898 "	July	1914

Certain other engines of both classes were similarly treated, as noted in the case histories. All the engines so treated had new cylinders, and piston valves. The fourth engine of the 'Dunalastair II' class to be superheated, No 769, was turned out of St Rollox works in January 1915, so can be regarded as part of the original McIntosh programme for these engines. The original and modified dimensions of the boilers of both 'Dunalastair II' & 'III' classes are set out in the table at the foot of this page.

The new cylinders were 19½ in diameter on both classes, and as rebuilt the only difference between the 'II' and 'III' was in the firebox heating surface and the grate area. The nominal tractive effort of both classes, at 85 per cent boiler pressure, was 18,315 lb, slightly less than that of the original 'Dunalastair III' class. The superheaters were of the Robinson type.

After rebuilding, No 771 went to Perth and was allocated at first to Driver T. Dalzell; they regularly had the morning 'stopper' to Aberdeen, returning with the first of the southbound express fish trains to Perth. The other three rebuilt 'Dunalastair IIs' went to Polmadie, primarily for the Gourock and Ardrossan 'fliers', on which the Caledonian was still in hot competition with the Glasgow & South Western. Their regular drivers were:

766	W. Cadzow
769	J. Butcher
772	J. Short

The engines had not been long in service before the last-named and her driver had earned immortality in the locomotive world. In the *Railway Magazine* for October 1915 Cecil J. Allen wrote: 'Coming on to the main down platform at Carlisle one evening a short while ago, with the intention of catching the 8.13 pm express to Glasgow—the heavy and popular 2 pm ex-Euston—I was considerably surprised to find at the leading end of the platform waiting to come on, not the mighty *Cardean*, but one of the original "Dunalastair II" class, No 772. In common with several other engines of this type, this locomotive has recently received superheater equipment. The contrast in size, as the London & North Western "Claughton" came off the train, and No 772 was attached, was indeed a striking one, and

'DUNALASTAIR II' & 'III' BOILERS

Engine	'Dunalastair II'		'Dunalastair III'	
Class	Saturated	Superheated	Saturated	Superheated
Heating surface, sq ft				
Firebox	1,381·22	1,094·25	1,402	1,094·25
Tubes	118·78	118·75	138	138
Superheater	—	214	—	214
Total	1,500	1,427	1,540	1,446·25
Grate area sq ft	20·63	20·63	22	22
Working pressure psi	175	170	180	170

Three 'Dunalastair IVs' ready for the Royal Train. The leading engine, non-superheater No 149, is the advance pilot. The second is a superheated 'IV', and the third a non-superheater 'IV'

the latter looked positively diminutive against the lengthy train of seven 12-wheelers and three large 8-wheelers, the tare weight of which was 375 tons, and the gross weight, with passengers and luggage, not less than 395 tons.'

The background to this affair was thus. *Cardean* had come south on the up 'Corridor', as usual; but at the time she was not long out of shops. David Stephen, not David Gibson, was driving her at the time, and on the outward journey he had been worried by a big-end that was inclined to heat, and a temperamental bogie axlebox. When he got to Kingmoor shed after the run he was convinced that to try and run the down 'Corridor' in that state would be asking for trouble, and as Jim Short was on the shed with 772, they were put on to the 'Corridor', while Stephen nursed *Cardean* back to Glasgow on his own. It was quite characteristic of locomotive working in those days that the driver of an ailing engine stayed with her. But reverting to Short, and No 772, such a load as 375 tons tare was far above the normal maximum for an unassisted 4—4—0 of any class, let alone a 'Dunalastair II'. It may be that in wartime, and at short notice, no assistance was available, but there is no doubt that Short took the sudden assignment with relish. In the latter days of steam it was perhaps difficult to imagine the sense of 'pride in the job' that permeated locomotive workings in the days of the old companies. At Polmadie the men who worked on *Cardean* were the high aristocrats of their craft. No one else got a turn on that 'train of trains', the afternoon 'Corridor' to Carlisle and back; and so instead of sitting back and demanding a pilot, or else prophesying the losing of time hand over fist, Short and his fireman rejoiced in their opportunity, and produced one of the most astonishing runs ever logged with a 'Dunalastair II'.

It was supremely fortunate that Cecil J. Allen was a passenger on the train, for his log provides data concerning Caledonian 4—4—0 performance that is of the utmost importance. It is fairly clear that some highly skilful preparation of the fire had taken place, because there was no gradual building up of the effort. The start was extremely vigorous, and up the two lengthy stretches of 1 in 200 from Gretna the sustained minimum speed was in each case 44 mph. Taking modern figures for train resistance, which would probably be a little on the low side, even for the superbly maintained West Coast Joint Stock of those days, gives an output of 955 equivalent drawbar horsepower. This is equal to a drawbar pull of 8,150 lb or 44½ per cent of the nominal tractive effort of the engine. In all the circumstances this was a phenomenal effort. In

8.13 pm CARLISLE—STRAWFRANK JUNCTION
The Down Corridor
Load : 375 tons tare, 395 tons full
Engine : 'Dunalastair II' superheater 4—4—0 No 772
Driver : J. Short

Dist miles			Sch min	Actual m s	Speeds mph
0·0	CARLISLE	. .	0	0 00	—
4·1	Rockcliffe .	.		7 05	—
8·6	Gretna Junc	. .	11	11 45	62½
13·0	Kirkpatrick	.		17 10	43¼
16·7	Kirtlebridge	.	21	21 50	56
20·1	Ecclefechan	.		25 40	44
25·8	LOCKERBIE .	.	31	32 05	—
28·7	Nethercleugh	.		34 50	66
31·7	Dinwoodie	.		37 40	—
34·5	Wamphray	.		40 35	—
39·7	BEATTOCK .	.	45	47 15	44 (min)
0·0				0 00*	
10·0	Summit .	. .	19	21 25	32½/27½
12·9	Elvanfoot .	.		25 00	—
15·6	Crawford .	.		27 35	67
18·3	Abington .	.		29 55	64½
23·5	Lamington .	.		34 55	66
27·2	SYMINGTON	.		38 50	54
28·8	Thankerton .	.		40 25	69
30·3	Leggatfoot	.		42 15	
33·5	Strawfrank Junc	.	42	Net 45¼	

* Banked by 0—4—4 tank engine

recent times various modern locomotives have been steamed to the limit of their capacity on one or other of the stationary testing plants, and at speeds of about 40 mph the maximum output that has been achieved has been roughly 40 to 45 per cent of the nominal tractive effort. That a 'Dunalastair II' put at little notice on to a crack train could have achieved the same result leaves one full of admiration. It might be argued that the boiler was mortgaged in the process; but from the way the engine was run from Lockerbie to Beattock one can hardly imagine there was any shortage of steam.

Thus, with this huge load, for so small an engine, only 2¼ min were dropped on schedule from Carlisle to Beattock. In his first description of the run Allen was inclined to 'write down' the rest of the journey; but on careful analysis the engine continued to do amazingly well. One of the standard 0—4—4 tank engines assisted in rear up the Beattock bank, and the circumstances may be compared to a run of my own, logged in the summer of 1932, when the 12.42 pm from Carlisle was taken by a Midland compound, No 1137. The load was 420 tons gross from Carlisle, and 475 tons from Lockerbie, after attaching the through coaches from Whithorn to Edinburgh. Out of Carlisle the compound had taken 27 min 5 sec to pass Ecclefechan against the

25 min 40 sec of the 'Dunalastair II'; but it was on leaving Beattock, again with an 0—4—4 tank engine in rear, that the comparison was so striking. The compound and her banker took 23 min 37 sec to pass summit, speed having risen to 27½ mph near Auchencastle, and fallen to 26, sustained, on the upper reaches of the bank. The 'Dunalastair' took only 21 min 25 sec, with the remarkable speeds of 32½ mph maximum and 27½ mph minimum. The subsequent downhill speed was no more than moderate, however, and nothing of the 2½ min lost between Beattock and summit was regained. The engine was going hard again from Lamington as remarkably evidenced by the minimum speed of 54 mph at Symington, and the very rapid rise to 69 mph at Thankerton. But the train was pulled up by adverse signals at Leggatfoot, and after the detaching of the Edinburgh portion there were signal checks all the way down into Glasgow.

The point that remains most strongly in mind over this remarkable run, apart from the actual engine performance, is that so small an engine should have been allowed to take so great a load unassisted from Carlisle to Beattock. From various documents that I have been able to study it would seem that the drivers, and even higher authority, did very much as they liked. This not only applied to taking very heavy loads without help, but in putting on pilot engines specially to help in regaining lost time. In 1908 a letter signed by McIntosh read:

'It has been noticed lately that there has been an increase in piloting express trains especially West Coast through trains. In some instances the reason for this step is not at all clear and Locomotive Foremen and all concerned are requested to examine carefully all requests for pilot assistance. It is obvious that at times when West Coast trains are late in arrival at Carlisle, it has been considered necessary to attach a second engine. This of course unless the load requires extra assistance should not be allowed to continue.'

More evidence that drivers were in the habit of working as they pleased is provided by another letter from McIntosh, on a later occasion:

'The increasing practice of drivers of down trains ex-Carlisle not taking banking assistance at Beattock must cease forthwith. The rule laid down for banking assistance in the General Appendix must be adhered to at all times, and serious notice will be taken of any departure which is unauthorised, from the rules laid down.'

The regular load of one of the most important superheater 'Dunalastair IV' duties, the 2.54 am 'Postal', was:

Brake van		
50 ft Postal carriage		Euston
50 ft Postal carriage		to
57 ft Postal carriage		Aberdeen
Six Postal carriages	Euston to Edinburgh	
One Postal carriage	Euston to Glasgow	

Load out of Carlisle 11, equal to 16½

A superheater 'Dunalastair IV' No 119 on Perth-Aberdeen stopping train near Luncarty

A superheater 4—4—0 No 132 at Perth, fitted with pop-safety valves.
Photograph taken in 1921

The Glasgow and Edinburgh vehicles were detached at Carstairs. At Stirling the Glasgow-Aberdeen passenger section was added. The 'Postal' was by far the hardest regular working. The purely passenger trains, though smartly timed, for the most part conveyed no more than moderate loads; six, equal to 9 or 9½ was a common make-up.

Before closing this chapter, mention must be made of the McIntosh spark-arrester, which was introduced in the early superheater days and eventually fitted to the bulk of the Caledonian locomotive stock. The arrangement of this device was thus: in front of the tube plate, forming a 'V' between the tube plate and the blast pipe were two vertical plates. Sparks issuing from the tubes struck the V-plate and were deflected towards the front corners of the smokebox. The cinders were pre-

vented from going up the chimney by means of sloping wing plates, which also assisted in the downward deflecting of the sparks. If any 'escaped' they impinged against a louvre on the inside of the smokebox door. As the ashes collected on the bottom of the smokebox it was found that they gradually moved back towards the angle of the V-plate where they cooled. Then they were raised by suction up a separate pipe and ejected as dead ash through the chimney. The V-plates were pivoted, and the deflectors could be folded down, so that they could be moved clear when tube cleaning was necessary. Although no inconvenience was thus caused in maintenance work, the presence of these deflector plates in the smokebox must undoubtedly have had an adverse effect on the steaming of the engines.

CHAPTER 7

THE PICKERSGILL 4-4-0s

A CHANGE of locomotive superintendent on any of the former railway companies of Great Britain could always signalise a change in design policy, and the Caledonian was certainly the scene of one such change, when John Farquharson McIntosh was succeeded by William Pickersgill early in 1914. The change in policy affected the 4—4—0 stud least of all; so much so indeed, that the Pickersgill 4—4—0s could certainly be considered as off-shoots of the 'Dunalastair' family. In many features of their design they were direct 'blood relations', as it were, whereas Pickersgill's 4—6—0s were a race, or a series of races, completely apart from the McIntosh inside-cylindered 4—6—0 stud. The Pickersgill 4—4—0s came to be so closely associated with the McIntosh superheated 4—4—0s that from the period immediately following the end of World War I the whole group of engines needs to be considered together. Although certain superficial changes in external appearance made the Pickersgills immediately recognisable from their predecessors the traditional appearance and finish of Caledonian engines was fully maintained. The changes in design, other than pure externals, were, however, enough to create a definite line of demarcation between the new and the older engines, and at this stage it is interesting to reflect upon the origin of those changes, as reflected in the personality of the designer himself.

The period 1912-14 was one in which there was a general change in locomotive superintendents on the Scottish railways. The first move was at the beginning of 1912, when James Manson retired from the Glasgow & South Western Railway. 'Sou-West' men felt that the natural successor would have been the man who had previously succeeded him on the GNSR at Inverurie, namely Pickersgill; he had made no radical changes in the north since Manson left, and Manson's work was held in such veneration down in the south-west

that Pickersgill was thought to be an ideal man to carry on the traditions at Kilmarnock. This was not necessarily the attitude of the railway management; but it was an opinion freely voiced in the locomotive department. Instead, however, the G & SWR got Peter Drummond, from the Highland, who proceeded to turn the entire Kilmarnock edifice inside out!

On the Caledonian one would have thought that the great traditions of St Rollox were such that a suitable successor to McIntosh could have been found among their own men. Robert Urie, who at one time would have been thought the natural successor, had, like many Scots engineers—and enginemen too—gone south to work under Dugald Drummond on the London & South Western. Two strong personalities nevertheless remained at St Rollox in Tom Weir, the chief locomotive draughtsman, and John Barr, the running superintendent. Weir had been in charge of the drawing office for more than fifteen years; but Barr was a younger man, and definitely one of the rising stars of the Caledonian. Tradition might have continued, and following the example of McIntosh, and of Lambie before him, a 'running man' might once again have been placed in the chair at St Rollox.

It is evident, however, that the appointment of a new locomotive superintendent was a matter of private negotiation once McIntosh had intimated to the board his intention to retire. The first mention of the matter in the minutes of the Caledonian board is on 9 December 1913, in these terms:

Locomotive Superintendent, Resignation of Mr. J. F. McIntosh.

> Agree to appoint Mr. William Pickersgill as Locomotive Superintendent at a salary of £1,250 per annum from a date in May 1914 to be fixed by agreement.

There had, of course, been some correspondence between the Caledonian and the Great North of

One of the first Pickersgill 4—4—0s, No 114 built at St Rollox in 1916

Scotland Railways before this, and at a meeting of the GNSR board, held on 16 December 1913, the following minute was recorded:

'Submitted—Letter dated 12th instant from Mr. Matheson, General Manager of the Caledonian Railway Company, stating that his Directors had resolved to offer the appointment of Locomotive Superintendent of his Company to this Company's Locomotive Superintendent, Mr. William Pickersgill. Remitted to the Chairman, Deputy-Chairman and General Manager to look out for a successor to Mr. Pickersgill and report.'

In passing, it is interesting to recall that the salary offered to, and accepted by Mr Pickersgill was less than two-thirds of what Dugald Drummond was receiving in 1884 from the Caledonian Railway, when he resigned to take up the position in Australia that never materialised.

Pickersgill thus took office in the spring of 1914. With the onset of war the Caledonian was soon faced with the need for new engines; but instead of taking the successful and economical McIntosh superheated 'Dunalastair IV' a very considerable amount of re-design was undertaken. Structurally, the '113' class, dating from 1916, represented an all-round advance even upon the massive proportions of the 'Dunalastair IVs', chiefly in regard to bearing surfaces. The following table gives some of the more significant differences. The reduction in

the distance between the centreline of the cylinders made possible the very substantial increase in the length of the driving axle bearings from $7\frac{1}{2}$ in to 9 in; despite the reduction in distance between cylinder centrelines there was still an opening in the frames, and through this protruded the relief valve connection from end to end of the cylinder, in the middle of which was the by-pass valve, of similar type to that used on the earliest Midland superheater 4—4—0s. They had the same very strong stretcher between the frames just in front of the firebox. Finally, the main frame plates were $1\frac{1}{4}$ in thick, against $1\frac{1}{16}$ in in the superheated 'Dunalastair IV'. From a study of these dimensions

CALEDONIAN SUPERHEATER 4—4—0s

Class		Dunalastair IV	Pickersgill
Crankpins diameter × length	in	$9\frac{1}{4} \times 4$	$9\frac{1}{2} \times 4\frac{1}{2}$
Driving axle bearings diameter × length	in	$9\frac{1}{4} \times 7\frac{1}{2}$	$9\frac{1}{2} \times 9$
Trailing axle bearings diameter × length	in	curved waisted $9\frac{1}{4}$ max $7\frac{3}{4}$ min	parallel $8\frac{1}{4} \times 12$
Coupling rod pins diameter × length	in	$5 \times 8\frac{1}{8}$	$5\frac{1}{4} \times 8\frac{1}{8}$
Centre to centre of cylinders	in	$28\frac{1}{2}$	$25\frac{1}{2}$

it would seem that the 'Pickersgill bogies' were intended to last for ever! The machinery was the same as on the 'Dunalastairs', with marine-type big-ends; piston rods forged solid with the cross-heads, and coned pistons. The ability to stand up to continuous hard slogging, traditional of Caledonian express locomotive work, seemed well assured in these extraordinarily robust new engines.

The boiler barrels were identical to those of the 'Dunalastair IV' class, but there was a considerable difference in the arrangement of the tubes and superheater thus:

SUPERHEATER 4—4—0 BOILERS

Class		'Dunalastair IV'	Pickersgill
Small tubes:	no	163	157
outside diameter	in	$1\frac{3}{4}$	$1\frac{3}{4}$
Superheater flues	no	24	24
outside diameter	in	5	5
Superheater type:			
first five engines		Schmidt	Robinson
remainder		Robinson	(entire class)
Heating surfaces in sq ft			
Tubes		1220	1185
Firebox		145	144
Superheater		295*	200
Combined total		1660	1529
Grate area	sq ft	21	20·7

* Robinson superheater

From the above figures Pickersgill would seem to have favoured a lower degree of superheat. The smaller number of ordinary tubes provided slightly more space for circulation of the water. The design of the pistons and cylinders was identical in the two classes, but a very important change was the use of 9 in diameter piston valves on the Pickersgills, against 8 in. The latter feature would suggest a freer running engine, while in the smokebox the diameter of the blastpipe orifice was $5\frac{5}{8}$ in against $5\frac{3}{8}$ in in the 'Dunalastair IV'.

Every feature so far discussed would suggest that the Pickersgill type would be an advance on previous practice, with the possible exception of the superheater. But experience on the Great Western was enough to show that one did not need a very high degree of superheat to secure outstanding performance. The undoubted fact remains, however, that the Pickersgills could not hold the proverbial candle to the superheater 'Dunalastair IV'. They were hard-working and long-lived engines, but they had neither the freedom nor the power of their predecessors. All Pickersgill's engines on the Caledonian were handicapped by their valve setting. The 4—4—0s were perhaps the least affected in this way; but one can only point to the sluggish '60' class 4—6—0s and those monumental failures, the '956' class 3-cylinder 4—6—0s, to appreciate that valve gear design was not the strongest point in the Pickersgill régime at St Rollox. Before passing on to a discussion of actual performance on the road in the early days of the class, mention must be made of the superficial changes in outward appearance. The chimney was a handsomely styled one-piece casting, and the coupling rod splasher was straight from end to end, without the upward curved portions characteristic of the McIntosh engines. Smokebox wings were dispensed with, but the most noticeable outward change was the abandonment of the huge bogie tender, and provision instead of a neat, but less distinctive, six-wheeler.

The development of tender design at St Rollox is interesting, as seen through the leading dimensions of four successive types:

Engine class	Coal cap'ty tons	Water cap'ty gallons	Length over frames		Weight in wkg order tons	Wheels no
			ft	in		
Dunalastair I	$4\frac{1}{2}$	3570	22	1	39·1	6
Dunalastair II & III	$4\frac{1}{2}$	4125	24	7	49·5	8
Dunalastair IV superheated	6	4600	24	6	56	8
Pickersgill	5	4200	22	1	48·75	6

Although reduced in length, the Pickersgill tender was nevertheless a massive job, and with the engine itself increased in weight from the 59 tons of the

Down West Coast express approaching Beattock summit, hauled by Pickersgill 4—4—0 No 79

Pickersgill 4—4—0 No 115 on the 1.30 pm up West Coast 'Corridor' express to Euston at Glasgow Central

'Dunalastair IV' superheater class to 61¼ tons, the all-up weight of engine and tender was still 110 tons, against the 115 tons of the preceding McIntosh engines. It is extraordinary to recall that a Pickersgill 4—4—0 with its tender weighed only five tons less than a Great Western 'Star'. The Pickersgill tender had the same wheel spacing as the Lambie tenders used on the 'Dunalastair I' class.

The first six engines of the class, built to order Y113, were completed at St Rollox in May 1916. They were numbered 113 to 116, 121 and 124. Engine No 121 took the number left vacant by the destruction of the McIntosh superheater engine of that number in the Quintinshill disaster. The first six went new to Kingmoor, and the original drivers were:

113	W. Telfer
114	W. Craig
115	N. Lawson
116	W. Todd
121	A. Craig
124	J. Veitch

It is evident from this allocation that these engines were regarded, by high authority, as being the 'last word' in Caledonian motive power. Todd, for example, had nearly always been on 4—6—0s and

had No 50 when she was new.

At the same time an order was placed with the North British Locomotive Company for a further ten engines of the class, Nos 928-937. These engines were allocated St Rollox order number Y118, because the material for the tenders was cut and machined there, and sent 'free issue' to the makers of the engines. The latter were built to NBLCo order number L664, at Atlas works, and they were all delivered in 1916. It is interesting to find that in an otherwise very comprehensive brochure produced by the North British Locomotive Company, covering its production record during World War I, the dimensional details of the tenders of these Pickersgill 4—4—0 locomotives are left completely blank. These Atlas-built engines were originally allocated as follows: 928-931, Perth; 932-933, Dalry Road, Edinburgh; 934-5, Balornock; and 936-7, Polmadie. The importance of Carlisle and Perth sheds in the working of the main line traffic was still very pronounced. Carlisle engines were then responsible for many of the Euston-Glasgow trains.

The Caledonian, as much perhaps as any British railway, suffered in its locomotive work from the effects of timetable deceleration, although the loads

Pickersgill 4—4—0 No 937, one of the batch built by the North British Locomotive Co Ltd in 1916

conveyed were certainly very heavy. One of the earliest published runs with a Pickersgill 4—4—0 took place in 1921, after the working of the 10 am from Euston was once again run in separate sections for Glasgow and Edinburgh from Carlisle. On this particular run, engine No 116 had a normal load of seven coaches, including a twelve-wheeled dining car : 235 tons gross behind the tender. The LNWR delivered the train into Carlisle on time, and the Pickersgill engine then had the task of taking this load over Beattock summit in 69 min, 49·7 miles. By the standards of early 'Dunalastair' days this may well appear as a pedestrian task; but in actual fact it was the first time since pre-war days that Cecil J. Allen had clocked an unassisted ascent of the Beattock bank. The start out of Carlisle was leisurely, with speed not exceeding 59 mph at the Solway Firth, and on both stages of the 1 in 200 ascent to Castlemilk siding speed fell to $41\frac{1}{2}$ mph. Lockerbie, 25·8 miles, was passed in 33 min 5 sec, but some rather brisker work followed on to Beattock station, with the ensuing 13·9 miles covered in 14 min 50 sec. The passing time at Beattock, 47 min 55 sec, was not heroic, by previous

standards; but the speed was 67 mph at the Annan viaduct near Wamphray, and something of a 'run' was clearly being taken at Beattock bank itself, as the station was passed at $50\frac{1}{2}$ mph after four miles rising at 1 in 202-174.

The ascent of the bank was again leisurely from so massive and potentially powerful a locomotive. But the train was on time, and there was no occasion for attempting anything exceptional or spectacular. After $2\frac{1}{4}$ miles of ascent, successive miles were covered at 32, 31, 28, $26\frac{1}{2}$, $25\frac{3}{4}$, $26\frac{1}{2}$ and $24\frac{3}{4}$ mph. This was by no means bad work with a trailing load of 235 tons, and in some places it would have been regarded as very good, with a 4—4—0 locomotive ascending a 1 in 75 gradient. But the Caledonian had set such astonishing standards in the past, that this performance, from a relatively new engine, inevitably pales by comparison. The complete ten miles of Beattock bank were climbed in 20 min 5 sec and the summit passed in exactly 68 min from Carlisle—1 min early. Then a most curious, yet characteristic feature of contemporary Caledonian running manifested itself. Although the wartime speed limits had long since been removed, this

One of the Armstrong-Whitworth built Pickersgill 4—4—0s, No 86; note the unusual type of number-plate

driver ran practically without steam from Beattock summit down the Clyde valley, barely so much as attaining 60 mph, until steam was put on nearing Lamington to climb the sharp ascent from the Clyde viaduct towards Symington. This train had a brisk, but by no means difficult point-to-point allowance of 17 min pass to stop, for the 17·2 miles from summit to Symington, and on this no less than 2 min 40 sec were *lost*. The train was thus all but 1¾ min late in arrival. Nevertheless, schedules were then so leisurely that a subsequent time of 43 min 50 sec for the downhill 32·3 miles to Rutherglen put the train ahead of time once more, though a final check outside Glasgow Central prevented a punctual arrival.

All the old downhill 'dash' of the Caledonian seemed to have vanished with the war, and it was rare even for the McIntosh engines to reproduce their former feats of speed, though as subsequent chapters of this book will show there was plenty of fine hill-climbing to be recorded. By the summer of the year 1921 another twenty Pickersgill 4—4—0s were at work. Ten of these, numbered from 72 to 81, had been built in 1920 to St Rollox order Y124, while the other ten were built between February and June 1921 at the Elswick works of Armstrong Whitworth & Co, and numbered 82 to 91. They were allocated variously, up and down the line, but it is remarkable that Polmadie did not receive a single one—not even of the final batch built by the North British Locomotive Company in 1922! There were, by December of this latter year, 48 engines of the class, and they thus became numerically much stronger than any of the different 'Dunalastair' classes. The allocation, as at the time of grouping, was:

Aberdeen	(6)	engines 70, 71, 80, 81, 84, 85
Balornock	(8)	„ 66, 67, 76, 77, 82, 83, 934, 935
Carlisle	(14)	„ 72, 73, 86, 87, 88, 95, 96, 97, 113, 114, 115, 116, 121, 124
Carstairs	(4)	„ 68, 69, 78, 79
Dalry Road	(2)	„ 932, 933
Perth	(12)	„ 74, 75, 89, 90, 91, 92, 93, 94, 928, 929, 930, 931
Polmadie	(2)	„ 936, 937

At this stage another early run may be mentioned, with one of the Carstairs engines, No 78, working the 10 am Glasgow-Euston express forward from Symington, with a load of 400 tons, gross, behind the tender. The 17·2 miles up to Beattock summit took 27 min 38 sec inclusive of a signal check at

Up fish special, near Cove Bay, Aberdeen, hauled by Pickersgill 4—4—0 No 85

Lamington. The minimum speed at the summit was 30 mph, after which the 49·7 miles down to Carlisle took 52 min 23 sec with a maximum speed of 71 mph at Gretna.

One of the most interesting of these early runs with the Pickersgill 4—4—0s was one logged by Cecil J. Allen, in the summer of 1921 on the 10 am up from Glasgow Central, with engine No 121. Incidentally, in his description of it he was evidently confusing the engine with the ill-fated 'Dunalastair IV', destroyed at Quintinshill, for he referred to 121 as a 'sister engine' to the McIntosh superheater 4—4—0 No 122. From Glasgow, with a load of 290 tons, the engine started well, passing Uddingston, 8·5 miles, in 12¾ min. Then unfortunately there came a dead stand for signals, so that the time to the Motherwell conditional stop was 25 min, 12·8 miles. The restart, up the continuous heavy ascent to Law Junction, mostly at 1 in 100, was not too good, as speed did not rise above 30 mph and fell to 27 mph on that sharply curved length past Garriongill Junction. The initial 5·4 miles to Law Junction took 13½ min and the remaining 17·2 miles to Symington, less severe, but still mostly adverse, took 25¾ min. At Symington the addition of the Edinburgh portion of the train brought the load up to 426 tons tare. An extraordinary relic of wartime conditions was that even in the year 1921 the load limit for unpiloted superheater 4—4—0 engines onwards to Carlisle was 440 tons, and so No 121 and her crew had to continue unassisted with a train that weighed at least 455 tons behind the tender.

From Symington 78 min was allowed for the 66·9 miles to Carlisle, in the proportions of 25 min for 17·2 miles up to Beattock summit and 53 min for the remaining 49·7 miles. After the adverse

*Down West Coast express approaching Beattock summit hauled by
Pickersgill 4—4—0 No 116*

immediate start out of Symington the engine got
away remarkably well on the falling gradient to the
Clyde valley, passing Lamington, 3·7 miles, in
6¼ min, at 55 mph. The ensuing 10·6 miles of
gradually rising track, mostly at about 1 in 300,
but finishing with 1½ miles at 1 in 148, somewhat
naturally took its toll, occupying 16¼ min, and the
last 2·9 miles up to Beattock summit, including 2¼
miles at 1 in 99, took 5 min 50 sec. The total time
of 29 min 50 sec thus showed a loss of 4¾ min,
and in relation to the load hauled it showed similar
characteristics to that with the Carstairs engine
No 78 on the same train with a load of 400 tons.
There seems to have been less in reserve for the
final stage of the climb with No 121, for her
minimum of 19 mph with 455 tons was not so
good relatively as the 30 mph of No 78 with 400
tons. Nevertheless one can imagine that the only
other 4—4—0 locomotives that would have been
called upon to perform such a feat of haulage as
that set to No 121 would have been the LNWR
'George the Fifth' class.

In pre-war days one could have expected that
an all-out dash for Carlisle would have followed,
to regain some of the time lost on the adverse
sections. But for the most part things were taken

very quietly. The ten miles from summit to Beattock
station took 10 min 20 sec, and the ensuing 35·6
miles on to Rockcliffe took 38½ min including a
slowing for permanent-way repairs between Kirtlebridge and Kirkpatrick. Maximum speeds did not
exceed 64½ mph on Beattock bank, 62½ mph at
Kirtlebridge, nor 67 mph at Gretna, and there was
a gradual fall away on the slight rise past Lockerbie
to 38 mph at Castlemilk. But although in post-war
days the Caledonian drivers rarely let their engines
really 'go' on the favourable stretches of line they
still used to run very rapidly into the station stops,
relying upon the decelerative power of the Westinghouse brake. On this run, for example, the last 4·1
miles from Rockcliffe into Carlisle took no more
than 5½ min pass to stop. There was good reason
for these brisk approaches to Carlisle, because the
last half-mile into the Citadel station is on a
gradient of 1 in 100 rising, which could be taken
in one's stride if the pace was still brisk at Caldew
Junction. If it were not, or if there happened to be
a signal check at the last minute, 4—4—0 engines
could be in trouble with these huge trains. I once
saw this same train hauled by a superheater
'Dunalastair IV' completely unable to restart from
a signal stop just outside the station, and serious

delay was avoided by sending the two North Western engines, that were waiting to take the train forward, back to couple on to the Caledonian engine and pull the whole cavalcade, engine and fourteen coaches, into the station. But to summarise the run of No 121, the total time from summit to Carlisle was 54 min 20 sec, or 52 min net, and a net time of 82 min from Symington.

After the pre-war working arrangements had been restored, and the 10 am from Edinburgh worked separately from the Glasgow, and ahead of it, the former train, conveying through carriages for Liverpool and Manchester, as well as for Euston, was booked non-stop from Princes Street to Carlisle, in the level two hours. A record exists of an excellent run on this train with engine No 78, and a gross trailing load of 255 tons. Out of Edinburgh there is a rise of 672 ft in the first 18·4 miles, and as the first 2·2 miles are level the average inclination in the 16·2 miles from Slateford to Cobbinshaw summit is 1 in 127. On this gradient engine No 78 averaged 37·8 mph—an excellent performance—

and Cobbinshaw was passed in 30 min 55 sec at a minimum speed of 34½ mph on the long 1 in 100 that leads to the summit. With such a good start no very fast running was needed down to Carstairs; the maximum speed was 67 mph, and the curve to Strawfrank Junction was rounded at slow speed, and that point passed in 40 min 5 sec from Edinburgh, 27·4 miles. This was followed by a fast climb to Beattock summit, covering the 23·5 miles in 27 min 35 sec, with a maximum speed of 67 mph at the Clyde viaduct near Lamington, and a final minimum of 38 mph at the summit. This resulted in a total time of 67 min 40 sec to summit for the 50·9 miles from Edinburgh.

Once again, however, the downhill running was no more than moderate. On passing the summit, 52 min 20 sec remained in which to cover the 49·7 miles to Carlisle and make a punctual arrival. And this time was spun out to within 5 sec. The time over the 31·1 miles from Beattock station to Gretna was 32 min 20 sec, with speed not greatly exceeding 60 mph on any of the long and favourable

Down stopping train leaving Carlisle, hauled by Pickersgill 4—4—0 No 69

down gradients. In its uphill work this was one of the best of the early runs with Pickersgill 4—4—0s; but they all seem to show the same pattern of performance: reasonably good climbing, and medium to sluggish running downhill. This was not a general Caledonian trait at that time; because after the immediate post-war period was over the McIntosh engines were running quite fast at times as the following chapter will show.

One is forced to the conclusion that the Pickersgills as a breed were not free runners. Mechanically they were very strong and reliable engines; no more convincing tribute to this can be found than their longevity. Under LMSR ownership if their repair costs had been high, and the evidence of mechanical failures on the road at all considerable, there is no doubt they would have been scrapped out of hand. But all 48 engines of the class not only survived to enter national ownership, but withdrawal of them did not begin until the year 1959, when the oldest of them were 43 years old. In the light of subsequent experience on other lines it should not have been difficult to make changes to the valve setting to remove that inherent sluggishness, and to enable full advantage to be taken of the 9 in piston valves. As things turned out, the design came to be condemned as of no consequence following trials on the Settle & Carlisle line in 1924. The work of engine No 124 in these trials is discussed in very full detail in Chapter 9.

Very shortly after the Caledonian Railway itself had ceased to exist, in January 1923 in fact, some coal trials were made with engine No 927 between Carstairs and Carlisle. The following details are taken from a letter to Mr Pickersgill from the Carstairs district locomotive superintendent, dated 19 January 1923.

One cannot be very impressed by these results.

4—4—0 LOCOMOTIVE No 927
Driver : T. Todd   Fireman : J. Paul

Date of Test	15.1.23	18.1.23	19.1.23
Load : tons tare 11.16 am Carstairs to Carlisle	156	162	187
6.32 pm Carlisle to Carstairs	201	205	206
Running time over 73·5 miles (min) UP	95*	96*	96
DOWN	100†	99†	100†
Coal used total cwt	70	75	82
Coal per train mile lb	53	57	62½
Water, total used gal	5603	5560	6095
Injector	Exhaust injector	Combination injector only	Exhaust injector
Weather	High wind	Fine	Stormy

* includes time of conditional stop made at Symington
† includes stop for bank engine at Beattock

The trains kept their somewhat leisurely schedules on each occasion: 96 min up and 100 min down, but with such moderate loads the coal consumption was very high, even allowing for the long time the engine stood idle at Kingmoor, usually from about 1.15 to nearly 6 pm. Furthermore, in view of past exploits one might have expected that Beattock bank would have been taken unaided, with tare loads of only just over 200 tons.

CHAPTER 8

GROUPING: THE EARLY STAGES

A VISITOR to Scotland in the years 1923 and 1924 would have seen little evidence of the change in ownership on the Caledonian line. In the late summer of 1923 indeed, in the course of some extensive journeys and train watching I did not see a single engine or carriage that was not still decked in the old colours, and when *The Railway Magazine* presented its usual annual Scottish number in January 1925, out of twelve Caledonian runs described in the 'British Locomotive Practice and Performance' feature the engines on no fewer than ten still retained their old numbers and livery, in the summer of 1924. The Perth Pickersgill 4—4—0s 89 and 90 had been repainted in Midland red, and renumbered 14494 and 14495 in time to work the Royal Train, on His Majesty's annual visit to Scotland; but renumbered and repainted engines remained in a very small minority. What is more, those retaining the Caledonian livery still looked as fine as ever in the blue. Moreover, the engines

of the Caledonian Railway had to work the entire traffic for the first two years of grouping. It was not until 1925 that the Midland compounds first began to work regularly over the Caledonian line.

It is of interest to summarise the position of the 'Dunalastair' family of engines as it stood in the year 1924, which was the last full year in which the former Caledonian engines had the line to themselves.

Class	Number of engines	State
Dunalastair I	15	Unchanged from original
Dunalastair II	11	Unchanged from original
	4	Superheated
Dunalastair III	11	Unchanged from original
	5	Superheated
Dunalastair IV (Originally saturated)	16	Unchanged from original
	3	Superheated
Dunalastair IV Superheated	22	Unchanged from original
Pickersgill	48	Unchanged from original

In the new LMSR power classification all the superheater engines with the exception of the 'Dunalastair IV' No 147, which had been super-heated while retaining her original slide valves, were placed in Class '3', and all the non-superheater engines in Class '2'. According to this sub-division of the 4—4—0 locomotive stock there were 81 Class '3' engines on the Caledonian line and 54 Class '2' engines. This meant that the 'Dunalastair I'

Euston-Glasgow express at Kingmoor, hauled by 'Dunalastair IV' class 4—4—0 No 146

Euston-Glasgow express at Beattock summit hauled by non-superheater 'Dunalastair IV' No 137 but fitted with the largest variety of bogie tender

class were now grouped with all their successors up to and including the non-superheater 'Dunalastair IVs'.

The general state of upheaval that followed the grouping within the LMSR is well known, and at first while the disagreements on future policy were being fought out south of the Border, the Caledonian was left very much to itself except that in 1924 train loadings on a tonnage basis were laid down for the Class '3' 4—4—0s as follows:

Down line:

Carlisle to Carstairs	320	tons
Carstairs to Stirling	374	„
Stirling to Perth	318	„
Perth to Forfar	402	„
Forfar to Aberdeen	318	„

Up line:

Aberdeen to Forfar	318	tons
Forfar to Perth	402	„
Perth to Stirling	318	„
Stirling to Carstairs	374	„
Carstairs to Carlisle	320	„

What the subtle difference between the '318' and '320' ton limit was I cannot say. At that time the distinction between speed timings of passenger trains into 'full load', 'limited load' and 'special limit' had not yet been applied to Scotland. The foregoing limits did not provide for unassisted working up the Beattock bank. Whether they applied to the superheated 'Dunalastair II' and 'III'

engines, which with their 19½ in cylinders had a nominal tractive effort little less than that of the larger engines, one again cannot say; but the non-superheated 'Dunalastair IIIs' were reckoned to take 50 tons less than the foregoing maxima, on each section.

In studying the details of many runs made on all parts of the main line during the years 1923 and 1924 one is struck by the consistent sluggishness of the Pickersgill 4—4—0s, whereas the McIntosh engines, and particularly the non-superheater ones, were frequently showing much of their old speed-worthiness when occasion demanded it. As a first example there is a run on the Glasgow portion of the up 'Postal', as from Perth southwards when a Pickersgill 4—4—0, No 76, had to tackle a train of 348 tons tare—30 tons over the LMSR limit. Excellent work was done to Gleneagles. On the first five miles out of Perth, on level and undulating gradients speed rose to 54 mph, and on the next stretch to Dunning, where the rise varies between 1 in 400 and 500, the fall in speed was to 49½ mph. Then on the bank itself—seven miles long, beginning at 1 in 121 and continuing at 1 in 100, the minimum speed was 27 mph. Thus despite the official overload of 30 tons the loss in time was only 20 sec on the schedule of 25 min. But then, after a splendid restart up the half mile of 1 in 100 to the summit of the bank the engine ran so poorly downhill as to lose just over a minute to Stirling—quite typical of a Pickersgill: 23 min 5 sec instead of the 22 min booked.

Two non-superheater 'Dunalastair IVs' on down Liverpool - Manchester Scottish Express near Rockcliffe, late in 1922. The leading engine has the smokebox wings removed

Another run, at the southern end of the line, again shows up the capacity of the Pickersgill engines on rising grades. Engine No 86 took a load of 330 tons unassisted, with a tare load just inside the 320 limit for a Class '3' engine. This time the speed reached as much as 69 mph at Nethercleugh, and Beattock was reached in the smart time of 45¾ min from Carlisle. But then, for some reason, in addition to taking a banker the train changed engines, and No 86 was replaced by a superheated 'Dunalastair II' for the rest of the journey to Glasgow. On two other journeys northward from Carlisle the engine was No 116, a Pickersgill; but the loads were heavy enough to require assistance

from the start—324 tons tare in one case, and 351 tons in the other. Whether any significance can be attached to it cannot now be said; but the fact remains that No 116 made considerably faster time when assisted by a superheated 'Dunalastair IV' than when assisted by another Pickersgill. Thus 124 and 116 together with a gross load of 350 tons passed Beattock station in 44 min 20 sec and stopped at summit in 62¾ min, whereas 123 and 116, with 375 tons, made corresponding times of 43 min 10 sec and 60¾ min.

Details are tabulated herewith of four runs with McIntosh engines, unpiloted between Carlisle and Beattock station, and in one case including a good

A Pickersgill 4—4—0, No 14488, painted in the first LMSR style, in Midland red, with crest on the cab side, and large numerals on the tender

Red engines on the Clyde coast : a 'Dunalastair I', No 14320 (old 730) in red, but still with decorated smokebox on Gourock - Glasgow express near Cardonald

unassisted climb to summit. The first two runs were on the 10 am from Euston to Glasgow, nominally non-stop from Carlisle, but including a conditional stop to set down at Motherwell. The non-superheated 'Dunalastair IV' No 136 fitted with the Weir feed-water heater, did well with the minimum load of this train—four 8 wheelers and a 12 wheeled 'diner' from Euston, and an 8 wheeled brake composite from Birmingham. The schedule allowed for a conditional stop at Lockerbie, which was rarely made, and with fast running past Nethercleugh and a maximum of 69 mph Beattock station was passed 3 min early, and summit passed 5¼ min early at 28 mph. The same engine also did quite well on the second run, with a 280 ton load, though on this occasion the bank engine was taken up to

LMSR (CALEDONIAN) CARLISLE—CARSTAIRS

Run No .		1	2		3	4
TRAIN .		3.56 pm	3.56 pm		3.30 pm	3.30 pm
Engine No .		136	136		140	46
„ Class .		D IV	D IV		D IV	MS
Load tons E/F		185/195	267/280		284/300	284/300

Dist miles		Sch min	Actual m s	Actual m s	Sch min	Actual m s	Actual m s
0·0	CARLISLE . . .	0	0 00	0 00	0	0 00	0 00
8·6	Gretna Junction . . .	11	11 00	12 00	11	11 05	11 25
16·7	Kirtlebridge . . .	21	21 05	23 00	21	20 45	21 45
22·7	*Castlemilk Box* . . .		27 25	30 25		27 45	28 20
25·8	LOCKERBIE . . .	31	31 15	33 35	31	31 40	32 10
—			—	—	34	33 30	33 50
34·5	Wamphray . . .		39 25	42 05		44 45	45 00
—				48 15BE	52	50 45BE	51 00BE
39·7	BEATTOCK . . .	48	45 05	50 05	55	52 45	53 00
45·2	*Greskine* . . .		54 45	60 40		65 05	64 30
49·7	*Summit* . . .	69	63 40	68 15	77	74 20	72 40
52·6	Elvanfoot . . .		67 05	71 35		77 55	76 05
63·2	Lamington . . .		78 50	81 45		88 50	87 20
66·9	SYMINGTON . . .	86	83 20	85 55	94	92 20	91 15
70·0	*Leggatfoot* . . .		86 55	89 20		95 20	94 15
—		pass	sigs	—	STOP	—	—
73·5	CARSTAIRS . . .	94	91 10	93 05	103	99 45	98 40

D IV = Dunalastair IV non-superheated
MS = Dunalastair IV superheated
BE = Bank engine Beattock to Summit

Evidence of the new order, down West Coast express leaving Carlisle, hauled by 'Dunalastair IV' No 14358 (old 149) and a Midland compound, No 1066

summit. Seeing that this engine would then have been reckoned as Class '2' these were very satisfactory runs on a crack train. Downhill speeds were moderate, but both trains passed Carstairs comfortably inside schedule time.

The third and fourth runs were made on the immediately preceding Liverpool and Manchester 'Scotsman' then leaving Carlisle at 3.30 pm. They provide an interesting comparison between the work of non-superheated 'Dunalastair IV' engines, with identical loads. True to form the non-superheater

engine made the faster start, beating the times of No 46 by a full minute to Kirtlebridge. But the latter engine was thoroughly warmed up and going splendidly by that time and her minimum speed of 50 mph at Castlemilk was absolutely first class. Both engines ran very well on the short stretch between Lockerbie and Beattock with times of $17\frac{1}{4}$ min and 17 min 10 sec for this 13·9 mile run, but the superheater engine, assisted by a Pickersgill 4—6—2 tank, made much the finer ascent of the bank, taking only 19 min 40 sec for the ten miles,

Edinburgh - Euston express climbing to Beattock summit hauled by engines 14352 (old 143) and 14484 (old 79)

Glasgow—Liverpool express near Beattock summit, with engine and train all red. 'Dunalastair IV' class engine No 14361 (old 926)

99

LMSR (CALEDONIAN) SYMINGTON—CARLISLE

Run No		1	2	3	4	5	6	7
Engine: 4—4—0 No		14507	116	96	135	134	14449	937*
„ Class		P	P	P	D4	D4	D4	P
Load tons E/F		304/320	305/325	315/330	329/345	342/360	342/365	404/435

Dist miles		Sch min	Actual m s	Actual m s	Actual m s	Actual m s	Actual m s	Actual m s	Actual m s
0·0	SYMINGTON	0	0 00	0 00	0 00	0 00	0 00	0 00	0 00
3·7	Lamington		5 55	6 05	5 55	6 30	5 55	6 10	6 02
9·1	Abington		11 50	12 10	11 40	12 35	12 00	12 05	11 50
14·3	Elvanfoot		18 10	18 55	18 00	19 25	19 10	18 50	18 02
17·2	*Summit*	23	22 05	23 10	22 20	24 00	23 40	23 05	22 02
					pws				23 37
27·2	BEATTOCK	34	32 10	34 00	33 45	34 00	34 00	34 30	34 52
32·4	Wamphray		37 20	39 25	39 15	39 10	39 15	39 40	39 37
41·1	LOCKERBIE	48	46 00	48 40	48 05	48 35	47 55	49 45	48 32
								pws	
50·2	Kirtlebridge	57	55 45	59 10	57 25	59 15	58 00	59 45	58 53
						pws			
58·3	Gretna Junction	65	63 25	67 35	67 35	67 55	65 50	67 10	66 57
						pws			
64·9	*Kingmoor*		70 05	74 40	74 00	74 50	72 55	73 15	73 45
66·9	CARLISLE	76	73 15	77 30	77 20	77 50	76 00	76 20	76 42

Speeds mph									
Lamington	max		61	61½	64	60	6	59	61
Beattock summit	min		39½	33	33	32	32	36	40
Wamphray	max		66	60	60	75	65	62½	70
Castlemilk	min		47	—	48½	—	47	—	43½
Gretna	max		72½	—	70	—	70½	74	68

P=Pickersgill type
D4=Dunalastair IV superheated
*=Piloted, Symington to Beattock summit, by No 777

against 21 min 35 sec. But both engines had kept their point-to-point schedule, and having matters well in hand both ran very easily down to Carstairs.

In the reverse direction the working of the 1.30 pm up 'Corridor' from Glasgow to Carlisle was a considerably harder task than in the once-legendary days of *Cardean*. Then the schedule was 135 min non-stop; but from 1922 onwards it was 129 min inclusive of a 6 min stop at Symington for re-marshalling. Out of Glasgow, the Liverpool and Manchester section was conveyed as far as Symington where a general exchange took place with the 1.30 pm from Edinburgh. The London coaches were brought together on the train leaving Symington at 2.29 pm, and allowed 76 min for the 66·9 miles to Carlisle, while the Liverpool and Manchester vehicles from both Glasgow and Edinburgh followed on a second train. From Glasgow the train was always heavy enough to require double-heading; but from Symington the London train was usually unassisted, and the engine that

had worked the 1.30 pm from Edinburgh took the Liverpool and Manchester train onwards to Carlisle.

Details of seven runs are tabulated for the London train with loads ranging from 320 to 435 tons. The apparent lateness with which some engines reached Carlisle was due to the train leaving Symington at the public time of 2.27 pm, by dint of smart re-marshalling, instead of the working time of 2.29 pm. The first run in the table, made in 1925, was one of the best I have ever seen on the Carlisle road with a Pickersgill engine. No 14507 was actually the same engine as that figuring in run No 3, namely No 96, and on both occasions excellent work was done from Symington up to Beattock summit, and the final minimum of 39½ mph by the engine in her 'red' condition was such as to be termed exceptional. It was rare for any really fast running to be made down the ten miles of Beattock bank, and drivers would continue to run almost without steam to the crossing of the Annan, just before Wamphray. The run of No 116, in column 2,

A non-superheated 'Dunalastair II' in red. Engine No 14329 at Stirling in 1926

was a typical Pickersgill effort, with a timekeeping ascent and then very sluggish work to follow. It was left to the McIntosh engines to produce the highest downhill speeds, and No 14449 (alias 122), in column 6, pulled off a very fine run with a load of 365 tons. On the last run Pickersgill No 937 had a non-superheater 'Dunalastair II' No 777, as pilot to summit, and did well thereafter to cover the 49·7 miles to Carlisle in 53 min 5 sec with her 435-ton train.

A study of these runs, and particularly those with the Pickersgill engines, show such consistent characteristics of good uphill work and slow running downhill as to suggest that a marked change had come over the whole attitude to express running on the Caledonian line. Cecil J. Allen hazarded an explanation that perhaps there was a growing dislike of high speed in Scotland; but this was not borne out by the smaller and older engines. Another

factor was that nearly all the most important turns were entrusted to 4—4—0 locomotives. *Cardean* and her three surviving engines, together with the two earlier 4—6—0s Nos 49 and 50 were rarely seen on the best trains, and no one who had any thoughts for timekeeping would put a Pickersgill '60' class 4—6—0 on to a fast turn. Many years later, in conversation, John Barr virtually dismissed the 4—6—0s as of little consequence in the working of the main line express traffic. As running superintendent he had clearly placed almost complete reliance on the 4—4—0s. Then, as described in the monograph dealing with the Midland compounds, these same enginemen, who seemed so reluctant to run hard, took readily to the new engines and not only drove them hard on the banks but took them tearing downhill like the 'Dunalastair I' class on the 'Tourist' express of 1896. This seemed to pin the sluggishness of the Pickersgills firmly upon the

A superheated 'Dunalastair II' No 14432 (old 771) as first repainted, in Midland red,
under LMSR ownership

engines, and not on the temperaments of the drivers.

Many years later I rode on several of the Pickersgills when they were still on first-class work over the Aberdeen road, and I found them most unimpressive engines. As I have told earlier in relation to the first and second series of 'Dunalastairs', they were driven on the regulator, with the lever about halfway between full and mid-gear, and the regulator about half open for the harder work. Like the later McIntosh 4—4—0s the reverser was power-worked, and if the driver let go of the lever it could move so quickly as to inflict a serious bodyblow if he got in the way. One can understand the men not using it more than necessary, and on the engines I rode there were generally only two running positions: halfway, or thereabouts, for level or uphill work, and almost full forward for easy steaming downhill. This latter was ideal for cushioning the action, and providing a steady descent without the need of frequent brake application, but in many cases it was too steady, and I remember one occasion when we were running late, and we glided gently down from Gleneagles to Dunning without exceeding 60 mph.

Two runs on the 10 am up west coast express from Edinburgh to Carlisle, clocked by Cecil J. Allen, make an interesting comparison, and contrast. One was hauled by a 'Dunalastair IV' of the non-superheater variety, and the other by a Pickersgill. This was the run briefly mentioned in the previous chapter. Although the loads were not unduly heavy this train was booked non-stop over the 100·6 miles to Carlisle in the level two hours, and with no opportunity of taking water intermediately the ascents first to Cobbinshaw, and then to Beattock summit, could prove trying, especially to a non-superheater engine. At the start there is absolutely no break in the collar-work. The line rises continuously from Slateford to Cobbinshaw, at which point an altitude of 880 ft above ordnance datum is reached. To Midcalder the gradients are 1 in 102 to Kingsknowe; 1 in 143 to just beyond Currie Hill; 1 in 134 for 2 miles past Ravelrig Junction, and then comes the only slight easing, with just over 2 miles at 1 in 220. Then after 1¼ miles at 1 in 120 there comes the final grind up to Cobbinshaw, with a solid 5½ miles at 1 in 100. Although the Pickersgill engine was slightly faster in getting away from Edinburgh, the 'Dunalastair IV' had caught up by Kingsknowe. On the continuous heavy climbing, however, the more powerful engine gradually drew ahead, and from Currie Hill her climbing was very fine, with an average speed of 37·6 mph throughout from Slateford to the summit and a sustained minimum of 34½ mph on the 1 in 100.

Once on to the faster stretches of line the 'Dunalastair IV' ran much more freely than her

10 am EDINBURGH—CARLISLE

		926 'Dunalastair IV' non-superheated 216/230		78 Pickersgill superheated 241/255	
Engine No					
„ Class					
Load tons E/F					
Dist miles		Actual m s	Speed mph	Actual m s	Speed mph
0·0	EDINBURGH PRINCES ST	0 00	—	0 00	—
1·2	Merchistin	3 40	—	3 30	—
2·2	Slateford	4 55	—	4 45	—
3·0	Kingsknowe	6 20	38	6 20	37
5·5	Currie Hill	10 20	37½	10 10	39
7·4	*Ravelrig Junction*	13 25	37	13 10	39½
10·1	Midcalder	17 35	41	17 10	45
11·3	*Midcalder Junction*	19 25	38½	18 50	45
18·4	Cobbinshaw	32 00	33	30 35	34½
25·8	Carnwath	39 00	71½	37 55	67
27·4	*Strawfrank Junction*	40 50	(slack)	40 05	(slack)
33·7	SYMINGTON	49 00	—	48 15	—
37·4	Lamington	52 55	64½	52 00	67
—	Elvanfoot	—	43½/52½	—	47½/53½
50·9	*Summit*	69 50	35½	67 40	38
60·9	BEATTOCK	79 10	75	78 55	—
74·8	LOCKERBIE	92 25	67/53½	93 20	—
92·0	Gretna Junction	109 00	69	111 15	—
100·6	CARLISLE	118 15		119 55	

The up 'Postal' leaving Aberdeen : coaches still in the old livery, engine No 14445,
superheater 'Dunalastair IV', in red

rival, touching $71\frac{1}{2}$ mph down to Carnwath. The Pickersgill came into her own again on the later stages of the ascent to Beattock summit, but having established an advantage of nearly $2\frac{1}{4}$ min at the latter point she went so sluggishly down to Carlisle that the train only just scraped into the Citadel station on time. The non-superheater engine ran splendidly, touching 75 mph down Beattock bank, running at 64 to 67 mph on to Lockerbie, and then clearing the rise to Castlemilk at $53\frac{1}{2}$ mph. Further free running down the long stretches of 1 in 200 descent, with sustained maximum on both stages of 69 mph, brought the train into Carlisle nearly 2 min early. The 'Dunalastair IV' thus gained nearly 4 min on the Pickersgill between summit and Carlisle —quite a characteristic performance on the part of both engines.

A few years later I had an interesting run over this same route myself behind engine No 68, Pickersgill, then renumbered 14499, on the 4.30 pm Liverpool and Manchester express, on which the hill-climbing was even finer, and the downhill work even more sluggish! The log of this run is also tabulated, and it will be seen that in a very vigorous start out of Edinburgh, with speed rising to $44\frac{1}{2}$ mph on the two level miles out of Slateford, we beat the times of No 78 on the London express to Ravelrig Junction; and although starting right on the grade from Midcalder we sustained almost as good a pace up to Cobbinshaw as No 78 had done

when taking a 'run' at it. This train had some sharp timings, and we did not keep them; but there was precious little of the old Caley dash downhill after Cobbinshaw had been passed. It was a day of heavy traffic and I was hoping for a big combined load from Symington. It was in the hey-day of the

4.30 pm EDINBURGH—SYMINGTON

Load : 240 tons tare, 260 tons full
Engine : Pickersgill 4—4—0 No 14499 (CR No 68)

Dist miles		Sch min	Actual m s	Speeds mph
	EDINBURGH			
0·0	PRINCES ST .	0	0 00	—
2·2	Slateford . .		4 33	$44\frac{1}{2}$
3·0	Kingsknowe .		5 50	$36\frac{1}{2}$
5·5	Currie Hill . .		9 55	$37\frac{1}{2}$
7·4	*Ravelrig Junc* .		12 55	41
10·1	Midcalder . .	$16\frac{1}{2}$	17 23	
0·0			0 00	
1·2	*Midcalder Junc* .		3 20	$30\frac{1}{2}$
5·2	*Harburn* . .		10 37	34
8·3	Cobbinshaw .		16 00	$33\frac{1}{2}$
—			pws	
11·4	Auchengray .		19 58	
15·7	Carnwath . .	$19\frac{1}{2}$	25 00	61 (max)
0·0			0 00	
1·6	*Strawfrank Junc* .		3 35	
4·8	*Leggatfoot Box* .		8 19	40
6·3	*Thankerton* . .		10 17	$54\frac{1}{2}$
7·9	SYMINGTON .	13	12 55	

THE CALEDONIAN DUNALASTAIRS

Midland compounds but the combined load would have been too heavy, and the first part, compound hauled, had only 255 tons behind the tender. I sampled this as far as Beattock, but there alighted and joined the second part, which was heavier and worked by a Pickersgill. It turned out to be one of the best runs I ever had with one of those engines,

yet even so including one piece of characteristic sluggishness.

The engine in question, No 95, then renumbered

6.10 pm BEATTOCK—CARLISLE

Load : 267 tons tare, 290 tons full
Engine : Pickersgill 4—4—0 No 14506 (CR No 95)

Dist miles		Sch min	Actual m s	Speeds mph
0·0	BEATTOCK .	0	0 00	66/60
5·2	Wamphray .		6 40	66
8·0	Dinwoodie .		9 20	68
11·0	Nethercleugh .		12 02	
13·9	LOCKERBIE .	16	15 10	
0·0			0 00	
3·0	Castlemilk Box .		5 38	45
5·7	Ecclefechan .		8 40	69
—			pws	30
9·1	Kirtlebridge .	9	12 27	—
12·8	Kirkpatrick .		17 18	61½
15·6	Quintinshill Box .		20 10	58½
17·2	Gretna Junc .		21 42	65½
21·7	Rockcliffe .	18	26 00	60
25·8	CARLISLE .	28	31 15	

SYMINGTON—CARLISLE

Load : to Beattock : 240 tons gross
to Carlisle : 205 tons gross
Engine : 'Dunalastair I' 4—4—0 No 728

Dist miles		Sch min	Actual m s	Speeds mph
0·0	SYMINGTON .	0	0 00	—
3·7	Lamington . .		6 10	58½
9·1	Abington . .		12 09	50
11·6	Crawford . .		15 09	50
14·3	Elvanfoot . .		18 41	48½/55½
17·2	Summit . .	24	22 30	40¼
—				77½ max
27·2	BEATTOCK .	34	32 15	
0·0		0	0 00	
5·2	Wamphray . .		6 45	68
8·0	Dinwoodie . .		9 20	63
11·0	Nethercleugh . .		12 00	69
13·9	LOCKERBIE .	15	15 05	
0·0			0 00	
5·7	Ecclefechan . .		8 18	
9·1	Kirtlebridge . .		11 25	66
12·8	Kirkpatrick . .		15 22	
17·2	Gretna Junc . .		19 15	71½
25·8	CARLISLE .	29	28 25	

Glasgow - Aberdeen express near Luncarty hauled by 'Dunalastair IV', superheater No 14452 (old 45), in red

14506, began with quite a brilliant little run to Lockerbie, with nearly 300 tons of train, touching 66 mph at the crossing of the Annan near Wamphray, and sustaining 68 mph between Dinwoodie and Nethercleugh.

The restart was equally smart, and we were sweeping down Ecclefechan bank at nearly 70 mph when we were pulled up for permanent way repairs at Kirtlebridge. The recovery was reasonably quick and we passed Kirkpatrick at 61½ mph; but then steam was obviously shut off, and we drifted down towards Gretna at less than 60 mph. There was a slight recovery afterwards, but it came too late, and because of the Kirtlebridge check, and signals slightly adverse at the finish, we dropped 3¼ min on schedule from Lockerbie to Carlisle. I am only sorry I did not take this second portion throughout from Symington and log the ascent to Beattock summit. The Pickersgill engine must have done well because she was close on the tail of the first

part on arrival at Beattock.

I have also tabulated details of another run on this train dating back to the early days of World War I, when it was still carrying a through coach for Moffat. The load was considerably lighter than either of the two portions on the day I travelled, but on the other hand the engine was a non-superheater 'Dunalastair I', No 728. The little engine did very well. Speed was held at around 50 mph, through the upper Clydesdale ascent, and on the level stretch beyond Elvanfoot it recovered to no less than 55½ mph. Beattock summit was cleared at 40¼ mph, and then there came a characteristic non-superheater dash down the bank, touching a maximum of 77½ mph. Continuing from Beattock, with a load of 205 tons, the running to Lockerbie was very similar to that of the Pickersgill No 14506. The finish, however, was much livelier. This was an excellent performance, and would have done credit to a 'Dunalastair I' in their early days.

Glasgow - Euston express near Beattock summit : a 'Dunalastair I', No 14312 (old 722), piloting a Midland compound, No 1148

CHAPTER 9

GROUPING : THE LEEDS-CARLISLE TRIALS

IN earlier monographs in this series I have told how the immediate impact of grouping was reflected in the motive power situation on the former London & North Western and Midland Railways. At first the Scottish constituents of the LMSR were little more than spectators in the struggle for supremacy that was waged between the combined forces of Crewe and Horwich on the one hand, and Derby on the other. To onlookers across the Border, on sheer weight of numbers the outcome seemed a foregone conclusion. George Hughes, of the Lancashire & Yorkshire, was chief mechanical engineer, and behind him was the massed array of some 600 superheated express locomotives of Crewe design, all equal or superior in tractive ability to the best the Midland could offer, in the fifty-five 4—4—0 express locomotives in the Derby No 4 class—forty-five compound, and ten simple. Scotland at first anticipated a development of Crewe practice as a future standard for the LMSR system. If it had been a matter only for the chief mechanical engineer things might have been different; but the general organisation of the new railway was based upon the

Midland pattern, and the superintendent of motive power was allied to the traffic side of the business, rather than to the engineering, and this key position went to an ex-Midland man, J. E. Anderson, who had formerly been deputy chief mechanical engineer.

An old friend, who had been a pupil of Sir Henry Fowler at Derby, once told me that Anderson, although a man of wide experience, had never been known to speak well of any engines other than those of Midland design. It was therefore not likely that he would accept the *fait accompli* of sheer numbers as a reason for standardising upon Crewe rather than Derby designs; and after the first strains of reorganisation had been taken up the celebrated series of dynamometer car trials over the Leeds-Carlisle line was run to compare engines of North Western and Midland design, of No 4 class, in general running, coal consumption, and so on. These trials, as they affected the Midland compounds and the LNWR 'Prince of Wales' class have been discussed at some length in previous monographs. But by the time these trials were

Typical of the Caledonian engines in the earlier post-grouping years : Pickersgill 4—4—0 No 14497, painted red, and kept looking very smart

concluded the Northern Division of the LMSR was getting into its stride, and the Caledonian and its locomotives had a very powerful advocate in John Barr, the new superintendent of motive power. The merits of the St Rollox stud were argued most forcefully, and on the grounds of maintenance costs, and general freedom from running troubles there was excellent basis for Barr's enthusiasm. Among 4—4—0 express passenger engines on the LMSR, the Midland Class '2' superheater of the '483' class showed the lowest repair costs, though of course the work they were engaged upon was relatively light. All-class figures for coal consumption and repair costs for five types of 4—4—0 were:

Railway	Engine class	Coal lb per mile	Comparative repair cost index
Midland	Class '2'	45·9	100
Midland	Compound	46·5	136
LNWR	George V	56·4	149
Caledonian	Class '3'	59·1	110
G & SWR	Drummond	63·4	147

The above figures are taken from E. S. Cox's celebrated paper 'A Modern Locomotive History', read to the Institution of Locomotive Engineers on 2 January 1946. Whether the Caledonian figures relate to all the Class '3' 4—4—0s, that is, all superheater engines—'Dunalastair II', 'III', 'IV' and the Pickersgills—or whether it applied only to the Pickersgills was not revealed. In any case they showed up well on repair costs, but not too well on coal consumption; though of course high coal consumption in itself is not an infallible index of performance. In early grouping days, for example, there would be no comparison between the severity of the work undertaken by the Midland Class '2' superheater 4—4—0s and the LNWR 'George the Fifth' class.

Be that as it may, John Barr urged most strongly that the Caledonian engines should be included in the comparative trials of different designs, and in due course Pickersgill engines were tested: a 4—4—0 between Leeds and Carlisle, and a 4—6—0 of the '60' class between Preston and Carlisle. Opportunity to test a 4—4—0 came at the end of 1924, when the outstanding success of the Midland compound No 1000 in the first series of trials had emboldened the authorities to test further compounds, on equal terms, against an LNWR 4—6—0 of the 'Claughton' class, then designated Class '5'. A series of trials was arranged between Carlisle and Leeds, on the same two trains as figured in the trials of the 1923-4 winter, namely the 12.10 pm up and the 4.3 pm down from Leeds; and as before it was intended to run with tare loads of 300 and 350 tons. Many of those intimately connected with Caledonian locomotive working felt that it was a great mistake to use a Pickersgill 4—4—0 to represent St Rollox; because all-round experience had shown that these newer engines were neither so powerful, nor so free running, nor yet so economical as the 'Dunalastair IV' superheater class. But of course the Pickersgills were the later design, and were considerably the more numerous. A number of runs were made over the route by way of road-learning with engine No 96; but the engine chosen for the dynamometer car trials was No 124.

Before discussing the actual work done it is important to analyse the duty set to the locomotives

Glasgow express leaving Aberdeen : a very heavy load behind superheater
'Dunalastair IV' No 14452

Participant in the 1924-5 trials : 'Claughton' class 4—6—0 No 2221 'Sir Francis Dent'

on these tests, particularly in comparison with what Caledonian engines had achieved in the past. The acid test of performance was of course the ascent from Carlisle to Aisgill summit, which in length and rise had some striking points of similarity to the ascent from Carlisle to Beattock summit. In the former case an altitude of 1,151 ft above ordnance datum was attained in 48·7 miles, while on the latter an altitude of 1,015 ft was attained in 49·7 miles. The two profiles superimposed upon each other make an interesting comparison. In the north-bound direction the Midland ascent of 14 miles almost continuously at 1 in 100 from Settle Junction to Blea Moor has no precise counterpart on the Caledonian line. Some comparison can be made with work on the 16 mile ascent from Slateford to Cobbinshaw, over which the gradient averages 1 in 130, and in the ascent from Uddingston to Craigenhill, where the gradient averages 1 in 120 for 15 miles. On the former ascent this book has already recorded an average speed of 37½ mph throughout the 16 miles, with a load of 241 tons tare, and a

sustained minimum speed of 34½ mph on the 1 in 100 section above Midcalder Junction. This latter would be an output of 875 drawbar horsepower. A similar effort with a trailing load of 300 tons tare would give a sustained speed of about 30 mph on a 1 in 100 gradient, such as that from Settle Junction to Blea Moor.

Looking now more particularly at the up journey from Carlisle to Leeds, the schedule time of the 12.10 pm train allowed 67 min to pass Aisgill, 48·3 miles. At that time the 10 am from Euston to Glasgow was allowed 69 min to pass Beattock summit, 49·7 miles, but on the latter booking it was rare for any load above about 250 tons to be taken without rear-end assistance up the Beattock bank. On other than test occasions the Midland load for a No 4 class engine over Aisgill was then 260 tons. The demands made upon the rival engines in ordinary service were not dissimilar, though of course in 1896 the 'Dunalastair I' 4—4—0s were passing Beattock summit in less than 55 min from Carlisle with loads of 170 to 180 tons! Comparison

Protagonist in the 1924-5 locomotive trials : the Pickersgill 4—4—0 No 124

One of the short-chimneyed standard compounds. No 1065 of this class worked in the trials

between the gradient profiles of the lines from Carlisle to Aisgill and Beattock summit respectively shows clearly why Caledonian engines had so frequently to be assisted, and to compensate for the stop for assistance and the subsequent slow progress up the bank the speed over the first 40-odd miles of the Caledonian run had to be higher than over the corresponding distance on the Midland. On these schedules the load rating for an unpiloted Pickersgill from Carlisle to Beattock was then 320 tons. It meant covering the 34·5 miles out to Wamphray in about 39 min, whereas on the Midland one could take about 41 min to pass

Ormside, 33·2 miles. On the really heavy part of the Midland road, the 15·1 miles from Ormside up to Aisgill summit, there would be about 26 min available, where the gradient averages about 1 in 118. From a flying start at Ormside the average speed required was about 35 mph.

From a forward analysis of the job it seems as though the Pickersgill 4—4—0 should have been able to manage 300 tons, at least. The starting allowance of 21 min for the 15·4 miles from Carlisle to Lazonby was very severe, and in no case was it kept by any engine hauling 300 ton loads either in the 1923-4, or the later 1924 trials.

CARLISLE—LAZONBY : 15·4 miles

300-ton trains

Railway	Engine		Time	Trials
	No	Class	m s	
Midland	1008 ,,	Compound ,,	23 18 23 16	1923-4 ,,
Midland	998 ,, ,, ,, ,,	'999' ,, ,, ,, ,,	23 05 24 11 24 05 24 15 23 23	1923-4 ,, ,, ,, ,,
Midland	1065 ,, 1066	Compound ,, ,,	22 28 23 28 22 06	1924 (winter)
LNWR	388	'Prince of Wales'	24 24 23 13 23 37	1923-4
LNWR	2221	'Claughton'	23 18 23 58	1924 (winter)
Caledonian	124	Pickersgill	23 51	1924 (winter)

THE CALEDONIAN DUNALASTAIRS

In this difficult task the Pickersgill 4—4—0, while not up to the best efforts of the compounds was certainly not behind the Midland '999' class 4—4—0, and generally comparable with the North Western efforts. It is unfortunate, for subsequent analysis, that the reports of the tests do not give the passing times at Appleby, and are limited to the overall times from Lazonby to Aisgill. Here the work of the Midland compound No 1008 was in a class by itself, while the North Western 'Claughton' was also being driven vigorously after an indifferent start. The work of the Caledonian engine No 124 can be more closely compared with the Class '4' simple engines, in the adjoining table.

Booked time over this section was 47 min so that No 124 regained 1 min, though the total time to Aisgill was 69 min 52 sec—2¾ min down on schedule. Against this the record of the Midland 4—4—0 No 998, Class '4', and a nominally more powerful engine with a much larger firebox, was not exactly brilliant. The total times on her six runs with 300 ton trains were: 64 min 28 sec, 67 min 18 sec, 69 min 29 sec, 70 min 33 sec, 68 min 08 sec, and 68 min 56 sec. Why this engine was put through so many tests in 1923-4 is something of a mystery. Her first effort was really splendid, but after that she was not holding her own on the uphill section, and her average time to Aisgill, on five trips, of 68 min 53 sec was only 1 min better than the first and only attempt the Caledonian engine and her crew were permitted to make. Seeing that the Midland engine was being worked by a driver and fireman who ran daily over this road,

LAZONBY—AISGILL : 32·9 miles
300-ton trains

Railway	No	Engine class	Time m	s	Trials
Midland	998	'999'	41	23	1923-4
			43	07	,,
			45	24	,,
			46	18	,,
			44	20	,,
			45	33	,,
LNWR	388	'Prince of Wales'	44	22	1923-4
			45	40	
			43	21	
Caledonian	124	Pickersgill	46	01	1924(winter)

In the 'red' era : Aberdeen - Glasgow express leaving Aberdeen, hauled by a superheater 'Dunalastair IV', No 14447 (old 119), and an identified Pickersgill 4—4—0

SETTLE JUNCTION—BLEA MOOR : 14 miles

Railway	Engine No	Time m s	Min speed mph	Max drawbar pull tons	Max dbhp actual
Midland	1008	20 43	33·1	4·2	902·5
	998	21 53	29·0	NOT ON THIS BANK	
		24 59	not recorded		
		21 21	not recorded		
		24 02	26·8	4·0	765
	1065	22 02	27·7	3·9	822·5
		21 28	30·5	3·9	825
	1066	25 00	26·0	3·93	748
		23 35	28·0	4·08	758
		23 05	30·0	3·75	725
LNWR	388	21 59	33·8	4·0	870
		22 50	29·0	4·05	920
		21 54	30·0	3·9	866
	2221	22 20	30·5	4·10	795
		21 55	29·0	4·10	840
Caledonian	124	24 55	27·8	3·72	680

and would be completely familiar with all its peculiarities, the effort of No 124 can hardly be described as a bad one. If some further runs had been permitted it is quite possible that some better performance might have been achieved. Unfortunately, however, while No 998 was run fast from Blea Moor, and easily regained the time lost on the uphill section, the Caledonian driver was not familiar enough with the road to take full advantage of the favourable lengths, and he barely held his own. His running time from Carlisle was 145¾ min against 143 min booked, and on account of checks the total time was 147 min 34 sec. For a Class '3' engine, competing against Class '4' and Class '5' units, it was quite a gallant effort, and not by any means the failure it has sometimes been considered.

The return journey on the 4.3 pm express was a harder proposition. The report does not give details of the running between Leeds and Hellifield; but with its incessant curvature, speed restrictions, and sharp gradients it is a section where a strange driver could lose a lot of time, due to over-emphasis of slacks, and lack of knowledge on the finer points of the road. Times are given only to Settle Junction, to which point the booked running time was 53 min. No particular significance need be attached to the Caledonian loss of 3½ min to that point, because the North Western 'Claughton' lost 4½ min on her first trip. The 14 mile ascent from Settle Junction to Blea Moor provides the real test of engine capacity on this run. In the trials during the winter of 1924 only one engine on one single trip kept the

point-to-point allowance of 22 min for this bank with a 300 ton load, while in the 1923-4 trials the times varied from a brilliant 20 min 43 sec by compound No 1008, to 24 min 59 sec by the Class '4' simple engine No 998. The complete record of performance on this bank, with the minimum speeds and power output, is given in the accompanying table.

On this ascent it is evident that No 124 was 'bringing up the rear', as it were, though her minimum speed of 27·8 mph and maximum drawbar pull of 3·72 tons were no mean achievements for a Class '3' engine. But she was not all that far behind the brand-new compounds 1065 and 1066. Before discussing the technical details of her work as contained in the dynamometer car test report it must be added that her mileage since last overhaul was much the greatest of the engines in the winter trials of 1924 thus:

Engine	Mileage since last overhaul
LNWR 'Claughton' 2221	23,825
LMSR Compound 1065	14,619*
LMSR Compound 1066	14,947*
Caledonian No 124	35,513

* since newly built

The dismissal of the Caledonian engine from the

scene after no more than one round trip was summary treatment, though perhaps to be expected in the circumstances. On the Midland line the regulation of train loadings by the Control system was very strict, and 300 tons was far above the normal allowed to a Class '3' engine. The operating authorities looked somewhat askance at the trials in any case, until the Midland Class '4' engines justified the confidence placed in them by keeping time with the heavy loads carried. But a stranger of Class '3' was another matter; and when that stranger had something of a struggle to get within 2¾ min of schedule on the up journey, and lost a clear 8½ min

on the return, one can quite imagine 'Authority' saying: 'We can't have any more of this Class "3" engine. Take her off.' Again, No 124 might have redeemed herself to some extent if she had run hard from Aisgill down to Carlisle. The times of her competitors, working 300 ton trains in the late winter trials of 1924, varied between 47 min 55 sec to 45 min 3 sec for the 48·3 miles from passing Aisgill to the stop at Carlisle; whereas No 124, passing Aisgill in 97 min 36 sec from Leeds, took 48 min 52 sec to get down to Carlisle. This of course was quite true to the normal Pickersgill form.

It is now necessary to set aside comparisons with

DYNAMOMETER CAR TRIAL RUNS
CARLISLE TO LEEDS AND BACK
Date: 26 November 1924
Engine: Pickersgill 4—4—0 No 124

	12.10 pm	4.3 pm
Weight of engine (two-thirds total coal and water) tons	100·0	100·0
Weight of train (with dynamometer car) in tons	301·6	300·6
Total weight of engine, car and train in tons	401·6	400·6
Train miles	112·86	112·79
Ton miles (excluding engine)	34,039·0	33,905·0
" " " " (10% added for passengers and luggage)	36,995·0	36,927·0
Ton miles (including engine)	45,325·0	45,184·0
" " " " (10% added for passengers and luggage)	48,281·0	48,206·0
Running time in minutes	145·75	146·47
Time including stops in minutes	147·57	150·42
Average speed in miles per hour	46·6	46·3
Maximum speed in miles per hour	70·0	71·0
Minimum speed on bank in miles per hour	27·5	27·8
Average drawbar pull in tons	1·86	1·74
Maximum drawbar pull on bank in tons	3·85	3·72
Total work done by engine in horsepower minutes	57,181·9	56,109·8
" " " " " " hours	953·0	935·2
Average drawbar horsepower	487·0	462·0
Maximum drawbar horsepower	675·0	680·0
Horsepower hours per train mile	8·41	8·28
Horsepower minutes per ton miles (excluding engine)	1·68	1·65
" " " " (10% added for passgrs & luggage)	1·55	1·52
COAL: Weight burnt in lb	12,310·0	
Pounds per mile	54·7	
Pounds per ton mile (excluding engine)	·181	
" " " " (10% added for passgrs & luggage)	·1668	
" " " " (including engine)	·1360	
" " " " (10% added for passgrs & luggage)	·1278	
" " drawbar horsepower hour	6·53	
Average rate of firing per hour in tons	1·127	
Average rate per sq ft of grate area per hour in lb	120·0	
Total time occupied in firing in minutes	1·70	1·69
Ratio of firing time to total running time	184·0	182·0
WATER: Gallons consumed	7,650·0	
Gallons per mile	33·9	
Pounds per ton mile (including engine)	·845	
" " " " (10% added for passgrs & luggage)	·793	
" " drawbar horsepower hour	40·5	
" " pound of coal	6·21	
" " sq ft of total heating surface per hour	10·08	
OIL: Motion: pounds used per 100 miles (average)	2·21	
Sight feed lubricator: pounds used per 100 miles (average)	—	
Mechanical lubricator " " " " " "	1·77	
Rape oil " " " " " "	1·27	

Glasgow express leaving Aberdeen in early LMSR days : coaches of LNWR and Midland stock, and engine No 14442 ('Dunalastair IV' superheated)

other engines and study the actual performance of No 124 as recorded in the dynamometer car. The accompanying table gives the complete set of data included in the report, and it will be seen at once that in addition to losing time the engine had a very high coal consumption of 54·7 lb per mile, and 6·53 lb per dhp hour. When the compounds against which the engine was tested were doing the job, and keeping time, on a consumption of 40 lb per mile, and about 4½ lb per dhp hour, it is not surprising that the Caledonian engine was 'counted out'. In its defence it might conceivably be argued that the engine was being fired on coal for which it was not designed, repeating the case made for the ex-Great Western engines in the interchange trials

of 1948. The Caledonian 4—4—0s certainly had small grates designed to burn soft Scottish coals, piled in thick. But the report states that the engine steamed freely, and her evaporation rate of 10·08 lb of water per sq ft of total heating surface was probably the best ever recorded over the Settle & Carlisle, down to the year 1930. For the size of grate the average rate of firing was astronomical, amounting to 120 lb of coal per sq ft of grate area per hour, and the evaporation rate was the highest of any engine in the 1924 winter trials working 300 ton trains. The Caledonian engine was making more steam than the 'Claughton' or either of the compounds, but her front-end could not use it efficiently. The evaporation in pounds per hour was

EVAPORATION : 1924 TRIALS

Engine	LMS Compounds 1065		Caledonian 124	LNWR 2221	
Date	18.11.24	19.11.24	9.12.24	2.12.24	3.12.24
Total water consumption round trip, gallons	5,700	6,400	7,650	6,560	7,315
Evaporation lb per hr	12,120	13,460	15,330	13,900	15,750
Water per lb of coal, lb	6·4	7·25	6·21	5·87	6·0

H

slightly surpassed on one of the 'Claughton' trips when the overall figure was affected by cutting the end-to-end time of the down run by a very fast descent from Aisgill to Carlisle. The comparative figures as shown on page 113 are most revealing.

So far as the comparison is concerned it should be added that the particular 'Claughton' was steaming badly, and that later trials with other engines of this class gave an evaporative rate of $7\frac{1}{2}$ to $8\frac{1}{4}$ lb of water per lb of coal. The figures for evaporation on the Caledonian engine tend to highlight the deficiencies of the Pickersgill front-end. Had some attention been given to the valve gear, a really fine engine could have been made out of the Pickersgill 4—4—0, with its massive frames, excellent steaming boiler, and 9 in diameter piston valves. As it was, the opinion voiced in the Derby dynamometer car was that it was 'the world's worst'! And in the ratio of work actually done to coal consumed, that judgment was not far wrong. While the use of a Pickersgill was inevitable, one feels that the results would have been much more creditable to the Caledonian if a superheated 'Dunalastair IV' had been used instead.

As an addendum, details may be quoted of two runs of my own at the northern end of the Caledonian line, in identical conditions on the same train in the same week. Both trains were on time, but in

LMS STONEHAVEN—ABERDEEN

Engine : LMS No		14470	14442
CR No		931	133
Class		Pickersgill	'Dunalastair IV'
Load : tons E/F		298/315	316/340
Dist miles		Actual m s	Actual m s
0·0	STONEHAVEN	0 00	0 00
1·6	Milepost 226½ .	3 55	3 40
2·6	„ 227½ .	6 00	5 45
4·6	Minchalls . .	8 30	8 20
8·0	Portlethen . .	12 15	12 15
11·4	Cove Bay . .	15 00	16 00
—		sigs	
16·2	ABERDEEN .	22 40	21 55

getting away from Stonehaven and climbing the two miles of 1 in 100-118 to milepost 227½, the McIntosh engine quickly established a lead over the Pickersgill despite an extra coach on the train.

The speeds in both cases were 30 mph sustained up to milepost 227½; but the Pickersgill engine was, for once, taken rather faster on the favourable stretches of line.

Glasgow - Aberdeen express passing Luncarty hauled by superheater 'Dunalastair IV' No 14451

CHAPTER 10

DISPERSAL OVER SCOTLAND

WITH the drafting of many new Midland compounds to Scotland, and the introduction of the 'Royal Scot' class 4—6—0s on the principal Anglo-Scottish duties on the West Coast Route, the Caledonian 4—4—0s began to pass on to less important tasks. First of all, however, some reference is necessary to the renumbering. The fifteen 'Dunalastair I' engines became 14311-25, and these were followed by the eleven non-superheater 'Dunalastair IIs', 14326 to 14336. Then followed the eleven non-superheater 'IIIs', 14337 to 14347, and the non-superheater 'IVs', 14349 to 14365. For some unexplained reason there was an isolated Class '3' engine, 'Dunalastair III' No 899, which had been superheated, interposed between the non-superheater series ending at 14347 and that commencing at 14349. This engine, LMSR No 14348, had been superheated in 1923, and apparently just missed being included among the Class '3' group at the time of renumbering. The superheater engines began at 14430, the original *Dunalastair 2nd*, and were as follows:

14430 to 14433	'Dunalastair II'
14434 to 14437	'Dunalastair III'
14438 to 14439	'Dunalastair IV' originally non-superheater
14440 to 14460	'Dunalastair IV' built new with superheaters
14461 to 14508	Pickersgills

By the year 1929 the 'Dunalastairs' proper were distributed as follows:

Shed	DI	DII NS	DII S	DIII NS	DIII S	DIV NS	DIV S
Aberdeen	1						1
Ardrossan	2	1		1			3
Balornock						1	3
Callander		1					4
Carstairs						10	3
Dalry Road				5	3	1	
Inverness		1					2
Kingmoor							
Ladyburn	8	1					
Motherwell	2			2		1	
Muirkirk	1						9
Perth							
Polmadie				2	1	3	
Stirling	1	5	4	1			
Stranraer		2		1			
Totals	15	11	4	12	4	16	22

Edinburgh express leaving Symington hauled by a non-superheater 'Dunalastair IV'

At that time the engines were still largely on their earlier duties on the Caledonian line itself. The 'Dunalastair I' class were mainly on the Gourock trains; a large batch of 'Dunalastair IV' non-superheaters had congregated at Carstairs, but

A 'Dunalastair I' in unlined black. No 14315 (old 725) in her last years

the superheater engines were mostly at the principal main line sheds. A single 'Dunalastair II', still non-superheater, had been allocated to Inverness, and there were three other non-superheater engines at Stranraer, for working over the Portpatrick and Wigtownshire line; but otherwise all were still at Caledonian sheds.

At this stage it is interesting to look at the motive power situation as a whole in Scotland on the LMSR. There was a gradual influx of new standard engines: Horwich 'Moguls'; 'Baby Scots', in addition to more and more compounds,

and Class '2P' 4—4—0s, and by that time also the LMSR managerial policy of reducing the number of different locomotive classes was getting well into its stride. Over Scotland as a whole there were still plenty of secondary and branch-line duties that needed good medium-powered passenger engines, and by their relative lightness on maintenance costs the Caledonian 'Dunalastairs' of all series were a better proposition than their counterparts from the Highland and from the Glasgow & South Western. With the spectre of strong 'Sou' West' supporters looking over my shoulder, I must say that in that

A 'Dunalastair II', No 14335 (old 779), in unlined black but still with bogie tender and retaining all the old dignity and grace of her type

116

*One of the superheater 'IVs' : No 14449 (old 122)
with the smaller bogie tender*

*A non-superheater 'IV' in the new age : No 14353
(old 144), unkempt, in unlined black*

particular period the various Manson 4—4—0s could not hold a candle to their hated Caley rivals. On the Highland the 'Small Bens' were good engines in themselves, but a little non-superheater 4—4—0 was becoming something of an anachronism in the 1930s. Scrapping had even begun with the 'Dunalastair I' class. And so, as newer standard engines began arriving to take on the heavier duties, the medium powered Caley 4—4—0s began to move farther afield.

In 1932 'Dunalastairs' began to appear at purely G & SW sheds. Hurlford got two non-superheater 'IVs' 14353 (144) and 14362 (927); Girvan got three engines, one each of the non-superheated 'II', 'III' and 'IV' series: 14335 (779), 14345 (896) and 14359 (150). In that same year the Perth contingent was reduced from nine superheater 'IVs' to seven of the same class, but as the engines displaced went to Aberdeen and were on the same duties there was not a great change. The most important point was

that by the end of 1932 no fewer than eight of the original series had been scrapped. Authority evidently intended there should have been nine, because 14316, old 726, was earmarked as withdrawn. But as previously mentioned, that old veteran, which had been at Aberdeen since its first construction in 1896, although 'dead' refused to lie down, and was still hard at work in the summer of 1934! Apart from those 'Dunalastair I' class which had gone at the end of 1932, the only other engine of the 'family' then scrapped was a superheater 'III', old 900, 14435, which was withdrawn in October 1928. She had been the leading engine of the down 'Royal Highlander' on the night of 25 October 1928 when it ran into the rear of a stationary goods train near Dinwoodie, and was damaged beyond repair. A non-superheater 'III', old 893, 14343 was scrapped just at the end of 1932.

By 1935, when the new Stanier 4—6—0s were arriving in considerable numbers in Scotland, the

A Pickersgill 4—4—0, No 14498, in LMSR lined black

'Dunalastairs' at Edinburgh Princes Street. Alhtough both engines are painted in LMS black neither carry smokebox numbers

strength of the 'Dunalastair' family had been reduced, by the end of the year, to the following:

'I'	class	nil
'II'	class non-superheater	11
'II'	superheater	3
'III'	non-superheater	10
'III'	superheater	5
'IV'	non-superheater	17
'IV'	superheater	24

Despite the influx of many new engines there were few changes. Hurlford and Girvan each got one more, but the remaining changes were small, and among Caledonian sheds. There was a slight disposition to remove the superheater engines from the crack main line sheds, and Kingmoor parted with its last two McIntosh 4—4—0s, sending 14449 to Carstairs and 14454 to Dalry Road. Aberdeen likewise had none after 1935, sending 14445 to Dalry Road and 14458 and 14459 to Stirling.

There was a good deal of very smart running to be recorded with these engines in the years 1929-33. Two most interesting runs were clocked by Mr W. S. Marshall on the Sunday evening Irish boat train in 1931, then leaving Glasgow Central at 8.2 pm, and running the 37·9 miles from Girvan to Stranraer Harbour non-stop in 67 min. The two non-superheater 'Dunalastair II' 4—4—0s stationed at Stranraer figure in these two runs, and although the loads conveyed were not heavy the route is one of most exceptional grading, involving the climbing of banks far more severe than anything on the Caledonian main line. It is, for example, difficult to imagine a more gruelling start than that faced by southbound trains out of Girvan. Right off the platform end the gradient becomes 1 in 54, and it then continues for nearly $3\frac{3}{4}$ miles to the summit tunnel, just beyond milepost 4. On the two runs tabulated engine No 14333 (old 777), on Christmas night 1931, took 11 min 50 sec to climb that fearsome 3·7 miles, with a load of 127 tons tare, while No 14334, with 151 tons, took 12 min 10 sec. These averages, from start to pass, of 18·7 and 18·2 mph were extraordinarily good for small non-superheater engines of 1897 vintage. Just how good they were can be judged by comparison with a run I had four years later on the afternoon express to Stranraer, when a Midland compound was working a load of 163 tons tare and the time from Girvan to milepost 4 was 11 min 53 sec.

LMSR GIRVAN—STRANRAER HARBOUR

Engine : No (LMS)			14333	14334
(CR)			777	778
Class			DII NS	DII NS
Load : E/F tons			127/135	151/160

Dist miles		Sch min	Actual m s	Actual m s
0·0	GIRVAN . .	0	0 00	0 00
3·7	*Milepost 4* .		11 50	12 10
4·9	Pinmore .	13	13 20	14 05
8·1	Pinwherry .	18	17 20	18 20
12·3	Barrhill . .	28	26 20	27 05
14·8	*Milepost 15* .		32 10	32 25
16·3	*Milepost 16½* .		—	35 25
20·7	Glenwhilly .	41	39 55	40 20
25·0	New Luce .	47	45 40	46 05
30·5	*Challoch Junc*	54	51 45	51 55
31·7	Dunragit .	56	53 55	54 10
34·4	Castle Kennedy .	61	58 05	58 35
36·6	*Stranraer Junc* .		61 40	62 10
37·9	STRANRAER HARBOUR	67	64 20	64 50

Down the steep descent to Pinwherry both 'Dunalastair' engines ran briskly, with speeds of over 60 mph between the slacks for hand exchange of tablets at Pinmore and Pinwherry, and the reduced speed of about 35 mph through the latter station made a bad start to the long subsequent climb to milepost 16½, high on the bleak moors above Barrhill. It begins immediately after Pinwherry station, on 1 in 67, and the gradients then average about 1 in 70 for 6¼ miles. The two 'Dunalastairs' averaged 28 and 28·8 mph respectively from Pinwherry to Barrhill, and 26 and 28·1 mph from Barrhill to milepost 15, which marks the end of the worst part of the ascent. The more

LMSR NEW LUCE—GIRVAN
7.30 pm ex-Stranraer Town
Load : 146 tons tare, 155 tons full
Engine : 14359 'Dunalastair IV' (CR 150)

Dist miles		Actual m s	Speeds mph
0·0	New Luce . . .	0 00	
3·8	*Milepost 21¾* . .	8 45	24
4·4	Glenwhilly . .	10 30	
8·9	*Milepost 16½* . .	18 30	35
12·9	Barrhill . . .	23 55	63 (max)
4·2	Pinwherry . .	5 40	65 (max)
3·2	Pinmore . .	8 50	23½
4·3	*Milepost 4* . .	11 00	
8·1	GIRVAN . . .	16 30	60 (max)

heavily loaded engine had done particularly well. After passing milepost 16½ all is plain sailing. The line descends steeply for over fourteen miles to Challoch Junction, where the Portpatrick and Wigtownshire line from the Dumfries direction is joined. There are severe speed restrictions for tablet exchanging at Glenwhilly, New Luce, and Challoch Junction itself, and speed did not greatly exceed 60 mph intermediately. But as the logs show, both trains passed Challoch Junction just over 2 min early, and the last stages, also with severe crossing slacks at Dunragit, Castle Kennedy and Stranraer Junction, were taken comfortably within schedule time.

Another run of 1931, details of which are tabulated, shows a non-superheater 'Dunalastair IV' in excellent form on the 7.30 pm up from Stranraer Town. The log, which in this case was compiled by Mr David L. Smith, starts at New Luce, and although the line is dead level for nearly half a mile from the platform end there follows a bank in some ways worse than that out of Girvan on the southbound run. Not only is the gradient 1 in 57 for three miles, but this section includes the notorious Swan's Neck curves, on which many an engine has 'stuck'. The 'Dunalastair IV' went up splendidly, not falling below 24 mph, and after the welcome 'dip' through Glenwhilly covering the remaining 4½ miles up to milepost 16½ summit in 8 min at an average of 33·8 mph. The gradients here are mostly around 1 in 100, and after recovery from the Glenwhilly tablet-exchanging slack the sustained speed was 35 mph. The maximum before the Barrhill stop was 63 mph, and this was followed by a smart downhill run to Pinwherry, 4·2 miles in 5 min 40 sec start to stop with a maximum speed of 65 mph. Then, from a dead start came the climb to Pinmore tunnel, and the summit point at

'Dunalastair II', No 14331 (old 775), with six-wheeled tender, at Ardrossan, in 1934

milepost 4. The gradient is 1 in 65-69 at first, easing to around 1 in 80, and it was certainly good work to cover the 4·3 miles to the summit in exactly 11 min with a sustained speed of 23½ mph on the 1 in 69. In this case, however, the climbing, with a load of 146 tons tare, does not compare with earlier 'Dunalastair' efforts on the similar inclination of Beattock bank; but the G & SW line train was on time, and nothing more strenuous was needed.

Another run logged by Mr David L. Smith, this time in 1929, shows a non-superheated 'Dunalastair III' on the Glasgow-Edinburgh route. In contrast to the one-time highly competitive route of the North British Railway between these two cities the Caley route was heavily graded, and consisted in the main of a single 'gable', rising to a summit point at Benhar Junction, 23 miles from Glasgow and 22·2 miles from Edinburgh. Taking the West Coast main line out of Glasgow Central, it was usually possible to get a good start to Uddingston, and crossing the Clyde at nearly 60 mph to take a 'run' at the very sharp ascent off the Carlisle road to Bellshill. But on this run there was a signal stop at Newton, and speed was only 33 mph at Uddingston. In the circumstances it was good work not to fall below 30 mph on the continuous 1 in 70 up to Bellshill. From the restart at Holytown the ascent is continuous to Benhar, on gradients mostly around 1 in 100 but including half a mile of level near Hartwood. Up this bank speed varied between 33 and 39 mph—again very good climbing for a non-superheated 4—4—0 hauling nearly 200 tons. There was then some brisk running downhill towards Edinburgh with an average speed of just over 60 mph over the 19·4 miles from Fauldhouse to Kings Knowe. The log does not give the duration of the

LMSR 9.50 am GLASGOW—EDINBURGH
Load : 181 tons tare, 190 tons full
Engine : 14337 'Dunalastair III' (CR 887)

Dist miles		Actual m s	Speeds mph
0·0	GLASGOW CENTRAL .	0 00	
1·0	Eglinton St . . .	2 50	
3·1	Rutherglen . . .	6 10	
5·0	Cambuslang . . .	8 30	
—		sig stop	
8·4	Uddingston . . .	15 30	33
10·9	Bellshill . . .	21 15	30
13·1	HOLYTOWN . . .	23 50	
2·6	Omoa . . .	6 25	
5·7	Hartwood . . .	12 05	33
7·4	Shotts . . .	14 45	39
9·9	Benhar Junc . . .	19 20	33
10·7	Fauldhouse . . .	20 45	—
15·6	Addiewell . . .	25 30	64
17·2	West Calder . . .	27 10	—
19·2	New Park . . .	29 10	60
21·8	Midcalder Junc . . .	31 50	—
23·0	Midcalder . . .	33 05	59
27·6	Curriehill . . .	37 40	60
30·1	Kingsknowe . . .	39 58	66
30·9	Slateford . . .	41 20	
1·0	Merchiston . . .	2 00	
2·2	EDINBURGH PRINCES ST	4 40	

station stops at Holytown and Slateford, but the aggregate running time from Glasgow to Edinburgh was 69 min 50 sec. The Newton signal stop accounted for at least 3 and probably 3½ min, so that the usual 70 min overall time from Glasgow to Edinburgh could comfortably have been maintained with two station stops.

Two runs of my own, into Edinburgh from the Carstairs direction, are also worthy of record. On

A 'Dunalastair III' superheater rebuild, No 14436 (old 901), in unlined black

A 'Dunalastair II', No 14332, rebuilt with '812' class boiler, six-wheeled tender, and raised cab.
With Pickersgill chimney and tall dome, the effect was horrible

both of these, with the morning Liverpool and Manchester express, the schedule was 38 min non-stop for the run of 27·4 miles. The hard work is relatively short-lived, and concerns only the nine miles up to Cobbinshaw summit. Although there is a mile of 1 in 102 to Carnwath the ascent is then

LMSR CARSTAIRS—EDINBURGH

Engine : No (LMS)		14455		14339	
(CR)		48		889	
Class		Dun IV S		Dun III NS	
Load : tons E/F		142/155		247/265	
Dist miles		Actual m s	Speeds mph	Actual m s	Speeds mph
0·0	CARSTAIRS .	0 00	—	0 00	—
1·6	Carnwath .	3 57	33½	3 40	37½
		—	56	—	45
5·9	Auchengray .	9 17	53	10 25	39
9·0	Cobbinshaw .	13 22	43	16 05	29¾
12·1	Harburn . .	16 55	58	20 05	62
16·1	*Midcalder Junc*	21 10	65/45	24 20	56
17·3	Midcalder .	22 43	—	25 38	58
		pws			
21·9	Curriehill .	28 30	53	30 20	61
24·4	Kingknowe .	31 20	easy	32 57	
26·2	Merchiston .	33 17		35 05	
				sigs	
27·4	EDINBURGH	36 00		38 00	

easy to Auchengray, and it is only in the last three miles that any stiff pulling is required. Here the gradients are mostly around 1 in 130, until the last mile which is at 1 in 97. On the two runs tabulated the engine power was in inverse proportion to the loads. The superheated 'Dunalastair IV' walked merrily away with her 155-ton load, touching 56 mph before Auchengray and clearing Cobbinshaw summit at 43 mph. With a subsequent maximum of 65 mph she was over Midcalder Junction in the smart time of 21 min 10 sec. The non-superheated 'Dunalastair III' hauling 265 tons had to work much harder. Speed did not exceed 45 mph before Auchengray, and the minimum at Cobbinshaw was 29¾ mph. But steady downhill speeds of around 60 mph were enough to produce exact timekeeping.

One of the best examples of McIntosh 4—4—0 running in that same period and, moreover, on first-class main line work, was a run I logged personally in 1930 on the 10.30 am up from Aberdeen with engine No 14442 (old 133) and a reasonably good load of 250 tons. Furthermore, it shows both uphill and level running closely comparable to that of a Midland compound, No 1143, that I logged on the 6.45 am out of Aberdeen about the same time, and which is recorded in my monograph on the Midland compounds. Engine No 14442 got away splendidly up the earlier part of the ascent to milepost 234 on grades of 1 in 118-154. The mile

121

A 'Dunalastair IV' superheated, No 14442 (old 133), in unlined black

LMSR 10.30 am ABERDEEN—PERTH
Load : 236 tons tare, 250 tons full
Engine : 14442, 'Dunalastair IV' superheated
(CR No 133)

Dist miles		Actual m s	Speeds mph
0·0	ABERDEEN . .	0 00	
0·6	*Ferryhill Junc*	2 10	—
2·1	*Milepost 239* .	5 00	40
4·8	Cove Bay .	9 20	33½
7·1	*Milepost 234* .	13 05	38½
8·2	Portlethan . .	14 25	51½
11·6	Muchalls . .	18 00	64½
13·6	*Milepost 227½*	20 15	48½/61
16·2	STONEHAVEN .	23 20	
2·6	*Dunnottar* .	6 20	31¼/40
4·7	*Milepost 220¼*	9 35	37¼
7·2	Drumlithie .	12 45	58
11·2	Fordoun . .	16 20	70½
14·5	LAURENCEKIRK .	19 45	
1·1	*Milepost 209¼*	3 15	41
3·2	Marykirk . .	5 25	63
5·3	Craigo . .	7 15	70½
7·4	*Kinnaber Junc*	9 25	57/60
8·6	DUBTON JUNC .	11 20	
2·7	Bridge of Dun .	4 20	56
5·8	Farnell Road .	7 55	47½
9·1	Glasterlaw .	13 05	34½
13·1	Auldbar Road .	17 50	55 (max)
18·0	FORFAR . .	23 55	
2·9	*Kirriemuir Junc*	4 50	56
5·7	Glamis . .	7 35	61/58½
7·9	Eassie . .	9 40	65
12·0	ALYTH JUNC .	13 40	59
16·7	COUPAR ANGUS .	18 20	61
18·9	Burrelton .	20 40	54
21·2	Cargill . .	23 10	64½
25·3	Stanley Junc .	27 25	53
27·4	Strathord .	29 40	60
30·9	*Almond Valley Junc*	33 25	
—		sigs	
32·5	PERTH . .	36 40	

at 1 in 102 past Cove Bay brought her down to 33½ mph, but there was a sharp recovery to 38½ mph on the last stage at 1 in 164 to the summit. We then ran briskly over the broken, though mostly falling gradients, and pulled up at Stonehaven just inside schedule time. Then came the gruelling start out of Stonehaven, where No 14442 attained 31½ mph up 1 in 92 to Dunottar box. Half a mile at 1 in 423 raised the speed to 40 mph and the last 1¾ miles at 1 in 102 were cleared at 37½ mph. A swift acceleration to 70½ mph at Fordoun brought us into Laurencekirk in 19¾ min to dead heat, to within a second, the compound No 1143 on the 6.45 am train. In my earlier monograph I wrote of this compound run: 'The sharp staccato of her exhaust on the banks, and the rapidity with which the driver got her away once each summit point was passed, showed clearly that there was little to spare.' Yet here was a superheated 'Dunalastair IV' pacing her almost to the second!

From Laurencekirk to Dubton again there was nothing in it. The relative maximum speeds at the North Esk viaduct were 71½ and 70½ mph and the time of 9 min 25 sec at Kinnaber Junction precisely the same on both runs. The Caley engine could afford to take things slightly easier on to Forfar, as the schedule of the 10.30 am train allowed a slight margin there, and on the 3¾ miles of Farnell Road bank, at 1 in 96-143 speed fell from 56 to 34½ mph. There was nevertheless a brilliantly smart start out of Forfar with Glamis, 5·7 miles, passed in 7 min 35 sec at 61 mph against the compound time of 7 min 40 sec. Once past Alyth Junction, however, the schedule of the 10.30 am permitted the driver to take things easily, and the average speed onwards to Strathord was barely 60 mph. Nevertheless this run shows clearly that a McIntosh superheater

The 'Dunalastair II' class engine No 772, as LMSR No 14433, as rebuilt a second time, in 1933 with Pickersgill superheater boiler, retaining original tender

4—4—0, well driven, could run a compound very

LMSR 6.45 pm PERTH—STONEHAVEN
Load : 315 tons tare, 335 tons full
Engine : Pickersgill 4—4—0 No 14489 (CR No 84)

Dist miles		Actual m s	Speeds mph
0·0	PERTH . . .	0 00	—
1·6	*Almond Valley Junc*	4 05	44½
7·2	Stanley Junc . .	12 15	38
9·4	*Ballathie*	15 10	61½
13·6	Burrelton	19 30	55
15·8	COUPAR ANGUS	21 45	65
20·5	ALYTH JUNC .	26 15	61½
24·6	Eassie . . .	30 15	63
26·8	Glamis . . .	32 25	58
31·8	*Forfar South Junc*	36 25	61¼
32·5	FORFAR . .	38 40	
2·3	Clocksbridge . .	4 56	45/55
6·9	Guthrie . . .	10 30	
2·0	Glasterlaw . .	3 55	45
5·3	Farnell Road . .	7 30	69 (max)
8·4	BRIDGE OF DUN	10 50	
2·7	Dubton Junc .	5 30	39
3·9	*Kinnaber Junc*	7 35	33½
6·0	Craigo . . .	10 35	56
8·1	Marykirk . .	13 05	45
10·2	*Milepost 209¼*	16 05	35½
11·3	LAURENCEKIRK	18 10	
3·3	Fordoun . .	5 25	53
7·3	Drumlithie . .	10 45	37
9·0	Carmont . .	13 20	50
11·9	*Dunnottar*	16 20	68
14·5	STONEHAVEN .	19 10	

close on a hard and fast turn, and makes one regret all the more that in the trials of 1924 over the Settle & Carlisle line that a Pickersgill and not a superheated 'Dunalastair IV' was chosen to compete for the honour of the Caledonian Railway.

About the best run I have seen with a Pickersgill on the north main line was one I logged in the late summer of 1930 on the 6.45 pm down out of Perth, when engine No 14489, then looking very fine in red, had a substantial load of 335 tons. She began well, accelerating rapidly to 44½ mph on the easy ascent past Almond Valley Junction, and not falling below 38 mph on the two miles at 1 in 125 up to Stanley Junction. From there, on virtually level track, speed ranged around 60 mph with an average of 61 mph for 24 miles and a maximum of 65 at Coupar Angus. The shorter start-to-stop runs north of Forfar all provided brisk starts, and downhill the engine was run faster than usual for a Pickersgill, with maxima of 69 mph down Farnell Road bank, and 68 mph before Stonehaven. Taken all round this was a most satisfactory run.

It is worth mentioning at this stage two runs on which the veteran 'Dunalastair I' No 726, as LMSR No 14316, was used as pilot, on heavy trains out of Aberdeen. She was frequently used to pilot the up 'Royal Highlander', in those spacious days when one could still choose whether to make the night journey from Aberdeen to London by East Coast or West Coast route. When staying at Stonehaven in 1929 and 1930 I used frequently to walk out into the country in the evening to watch the two London

LMSR : ABERDEEN—STONEHAVEN

'Dunalastair I' 4—4—0 No 14316 (CR No 726) as pilot

		1127 Compound 332/355		14503 Pickersgill 347/365	
Train engine No					
„ Class					
Load tons E/F					
Dist miles		Actual m s	Speeds mph	Actual m s	Speeds mph
0·0	ABERDEEN	0 00	—	0 00	—
0·6	*Ferryhill Junction* . . .	2 07	—	2 10	—
2·1	*Milepost 239*	—	40½	4 50	39
4·8	Cove Bay	8 53	37	9 25	31¾
7·1	*Milepost 234*	12 10	43½	13 20	37½
11·6	Muchalls	16 48	69	18 15	62½
13·6	*Milepost 227½*	18 42	58	20 30	49½
—		pws	—		
16·2	STONEHAVEN	22 02		23 35	62

sleepers climbing Fetteresso bank. The East Coast came first, and usually made the Stonehaven conditional stop, from which an 'Atlantic' and a 'Scott' would be roaring their hearts out up the bank. Then would come the Euston train, sweeping through Stonehaven at 65-70 mph. The train engine was always a compound, working through to Carlisle, and leading the way was little 14316.

I have thought it worth while tabulating two runs on which this engine acted as pilot, one assisting a Pickersgill and the other ahead of a Midland compound on which I was riding. On the latter occasion we could see from the train engine that the 'Dunalastair' was not being worked hard, and I think a division of the load in the ratio of about two to one would be fair. On the compound run we made a considerably faster climb to milepost 234 than with the Pickersgill. After Stonehaven the ascent of Fetteresso bank was a little faster than that of the unaided McIntosh engine No 14442; but once again past Drumlithie the driver of the 'Dunalastair' shut off steam altogether and our maximum speed of 64½ mph at Fordoun was achieved with the compound hauling the train as well as pushing her pilot!

A final experience of this same period was a run

A superheater 'Dunalastair III', No 14434, allocated to the Highland line, and fitted with small snowplough

on the footplate of a Pickersgill working the 10 am from Glasgow, as from Perth forward. We had no more than a moderate load, totalling 275 tons behind the tender, but the performance was not very inspiring. The engine was thumped along, but did not seem to have any real speed in her, and did not do so well as the sister engine No 14489 on the 6.45 pm from Perth, particularly in the disappointingly sluggish work on the level between Stanley Junction and Forfar. The engine steamed freely, and overall time was kept from Perth to

Aberdeen, partly by economy on some station stopping times; but it was not an impressive performance. The regulator handle stood about halfway over on the quadrant for the harder work, and the lever was mostly in the sixth notch from full gear, about 35 per cent cut-off. The accompanying log sets out details of the times and speeds made, and they are interesting only as a record of a footplate journey rather than anything outstanding in the way of performance. To me, however, it remains a fascinating experience.

LMSR 11.37 am PERTH—ABERDEEN
Load : 259 tons tare, 275 tons full
Engine : Pickersgill 4—4—0 No 14495 (CR No 89)

Dist miles		Sch min	Actual m s	Speeds mph
0·0	PERTH	0	0 00	—
1·6	Almond Valley Junction	4	4 47	—
5·1	Strathord		9 01	44
7·2	Stanley Junction	11	12 02	39
9·4	Ballathie		14 53	61½
13·6	Burrelton		19 37	47*
15·8	COUPAR ANGUS	21	22 30	
4·7	ALYTH JUNCTION	5	6 47	55
8·8	Eassie		11 05	58
11·0	Glamis		13 23	53
16·0	Forfar South Junction	17	18 43	58½
16·7	FORFAR	18	20 00	
2·3	Clocksbridge		4 30	47½
6·9	Guthrie	9	9 34	63½/51
12·2	Farnell Road		14 55	67
15·3	BRIDGE OF DUN	19	18 25	
2·7	Dubton Junction	5	5 11	39
3·9	Kinnaber Junction	7	7 05	37
6·0	Craigo		9 53	54½
8·1	Marykirk		12 25	46½
10·2	Milepost 209¼		15 29	36
11·3	LAURENCEKIRK	17	17 43	
3·3	Fordoun	6	5 42	
4·0	Drumlithie		7 11	39½
5·7	Carmout		9 37	48½
8·6	Dunnottar		12 42	60
11·2	STONEHAVEN	16	15 57	
2·6	Milepost 227½		5 33	32
4·6	Muchalls		8 05	58
8·0	Portlethan		12 05	44
11·4	Cove Bay		15 51	64½
15·6	Ferryhill Junction	19	20 31	
—			sigs	
16·2	ABERDEEN	22	22 23	

* Damper slipped out of adjustment : pressure dropped momentarily to 125 psi

CHAPTER 11

POST-WAR AND FINALE

THE 'Dunalastairs' as a family survived World War I with only one casualty, the ill-fated 121, destroyed at Quintinshill. The Pickersgills were born during the war and became the standard Caledonian express passenger engine class afterwards. They may not have been brilliant performers by earlier standards, but their quality as general utility engines was conclusively shown by their longevity, in an age when many engine classes with far more glittering records of achievement in express train working went rapidly to the scrapyard. By midsummer 1945 a roll-call of the 'Dunalastair' family gave the following results:

'I'	class	none surviving
'II'	non-superheater	2
'II'	superheater	none
'III'	non-superheater	4
'III'	superheater	1
'IV'	non-superheater	2
'IV'	superheater	23

Thus of the earlier varieties there were few survivors, but the superheater 'IV' series was still intact, except of course for No 121. Engine No 14442 (old 133) was to be scrapped in July 1946, but withdrawal of the remainder did not begin until October 1952, and the last one, No 54441 (old 132), was not withdrawn until May 1959, after a life of forty-eight years. Except for No 14481 (old 76), the Pickersgills as a class remained intact until May 1959 when 54461 (old 113) was scrapped. The Pickersgills did not have such long lives as the 'Dunalastair' superheater 'IVs'; the longest span was forty-six years by 54463 (old 115), which was also the last to go, and the shortest, excepting No 14481, thirty-seven years, by some of the 1922 batch built by the North British Locomotive Company Ltd.

At the end of the war the allocation of the superheater 'Dunalastair IVs' was as follows:

Carstairs	4
Dalry Road	3
Forfar	2
Ladyburn	5
Motherwell	1
Perth	3
Polmadie	4
Stirling	1

The other surviving 'Dunalastairs' in service were distributed thus:

Aviemore:	14338 'III' non-superheated	: Old 888
	14434 'III' superheated	: Old 894
Forres:	14333 'II' non-superheated	: Old 777
	14337 'III' non-superheated	: Old 887
Inverness:	14332 'II' non-superheated	: Old 776
	14340 'III' non-superheated	: Old 890

At that time there were also two non-superheater 'Dunalastair IVs' in existence, namely 14350 and 14363. These two were last working from Carstairs and Corkerhill respectively; but in 1945 both would appear to have been in store.

In 1945 the allocation of the Pickersgills was as follows:

Balornock	6
Carstairs	9
Dalry Road	2
Forfar	1
Hamilton	1
Hurlford	2
Ladyburn	6
Motherwell	5
Perth	11
Polmadie	1
Stirling	4

From this it will be seen that the majority of the Caledonian superheater 4—4—0 engines were still working in old Caledonian territory in 1945. The

*Train from Aberdeen approaching Millburn Junction, Inverness, hauled by
Pickersgill 4—4—0 No 54487*

only exceptions were two on the former G & SWR line, at Hurlford, and one, a superheater 'III', at Aviemore. By the time nationalisation had taken place there had been some migration among the superheater 'IVs' with three of them transferring to Dumfries, one to Aviemore, one to Inverness, and one to Muirkirk.

The most unexpected event in the later history of the Pickersgills took place soon after nationalisation, when the celebrated series of interchange trials in the early summer of 1948 included working the 4 pm from Perth to Inverness. The specified load was beyond the unaided capacity of any of the competing engines on the ascent from Blair Atholl to Dalnaspidal and rear-end banking assistance was needed. Several Pickersgill 4—4—0s nominally

*South express (via Forres) leaving Inverness with a Pickersgill 4—4—0, No 54496, piloting a
Stanier 'Black Five'*

attached to Perth were then stationed at Blair Atholl for banking work, and these engines played no small part in the making of some spectacular ascents of 'The Hill'. The dynamometer car registered the power outputs of the various train engines, and from the official report it is possible to calculate how the load was being shared, and what the power output of the bank engine was. The 4 pm train from Perth made passenger stops at Struan and Dalnaspidal, and the bank engines were coupled on to the rear of the train. In earlier days, with trains that stopped at Dalnaspidal it was more usual to couple the bank engine as a pilot in front, but during the interchange trials the assistant engine had obviously to be in rear so that the dynamometer car would record only the work of the train engine. During the interchange trials the work of engines 54499 and 14501, as they were then numbered, was recorded; but I have also a personal record of No 14467 doing similar duty in 1950.

In ordinary working, performance on 'The Hill', with Stanier 'Black Fives' as train engines and Pickersgills to assist, was very standardised. With loads of 350 to 450 tons the sustained speed on the 1 in 70 gradient always seemed to settle down to 26 or 27 mph, which was all that was necessary to keep the schedule time of a train like the 12 noon from Perth—allowed 34 min to pass Dalnaspidal, 15·7 miles from the start at Blair Atholl. On that train the banker was not coupled, and used to drop behind on passing Dalnaspidal. On two typical runs first with No 44998 in front, 14467 in rear and 375 tons, and second with No 44799, 14501 and 440 tons, the times to passing Dalnaspidal were 33 min 30 sec and 32 min 23 sec with minimum sustained speeds of 26 mph in each case. During the interchange trials the work of the 'Black Five' No 44973 was true to tradition, and her speed up 'The Hill' with a load of 353 tons was 27½ mph. The report of the trials gives the following details of performance, with Pickersgill 4—4—0s in the rear in each case:

Date of run	Engine class	Load tons tare	Sustained dbhp (actual)	Speed mph	Duration of effort min
6/7/48	LMR Class '5'	353	600	27½	22
13/7/48	SR West Country	360	1115	36¼	16½
22/7/48	ER 'B1' 4—6—0	352	800	31½	18

The maximum load permitted to an unassisted

Class '5' 4—6—0 on 'The Hill' was 255 tons tare, so that in the last-mentioned instance No 44799 was just about up to the limit.

In this book, however, I am concerned with the Pickersgill 4—4—0s, and there are five recorded examples of their work on this formidable Highland bank.

INTERCHANGE TRIALS

Train engine Type	Total gross load tons	Load taken by train engine	Load taken by bank engine
LMS Class '5'	375	225	150
Southern 4-6-2	380	310	70
ER 'B1' 4-6-0	375	260	115

SERVICE RUNS ON 12 NOON ex-PERTH

Train engine Class '5' No	Total gross load tons	Load taken by train engine	Load taken by bank engine
44998	375	225	150
44799	440	260	180

Taking the British Railways values for train resistance enables one to calculate the actual proportion of the loads that the train engine and bank engine were taking in each case, and in doing this I have assessed the gross loads as 375 tons for the two 4—6—0s, and 380 tons for the Southern 'Pacific'. In connection with the latter there was a story that went the rounds at the time, that the Nine Elms driver on engine No 34004 started from Blair Atholl with such vigour that he ran the bank engine out of steam before Struan. Certainly the visitor took far more than the usual share of the load, as can be seen from the following results of calculation:

Engine No	Load tons	Speed mph	Equivalent dbhp
unknown	150	27½	655
14501	70	36¼	595
54499	115	31½	645
14467	150	26	620
14501	180	27	725

The equivalent drawbar horsepowers of the 4—6—0s in the interchange trials were 890 for the

The down car-sleeper train, Kings Cross to Inverness, two miles north of Aviemore :
a Pickersgill 4—4—0, No 54484, piloting a Stanier 'Black Five'

Train of locomotive coal for Inverness, climbing to Slochd summit : a Pickersgill 4—4—0,
No 54482, piloting a Stanier 'Black Five'

J

SIX STYLES OF BRITISH RAILWAYS PAINTING

A superheater 'IV', No 54460, with small BR crest

One of the last 'Dunalastairs' : No 54458 at Dingwall 1956

A Pickersgill 4—4—0, No 54495, at Helmsdale 1960, with large BR crest

A superheater 'IV', No 54438, with no name at all, in plain black

A superheater 'IV', No 54455, in plain black with BRITISH RAILWAYS in block letters

The first style of lined black, on Pickersgill 4—4—0 No 54475

Stanier Class '5' and 1,130 with the 'B1'. The Southern 'West Country' 4—6—2 was making an altogether exceptional effort, though the effort might not have been quite so spectacular in bad weather. Reverting to the Pickersgills, however, their efforts were certainly not to be despised. In the trials on the Settle & Carlisle line in 1924, when No 124 was extended to her limit on the heavy banks, an actual drawbar horsepower of 680 was recorded at $27\frac{1}{2}$ mph on a 1 in 100 gradient. The equivalent figure for level track would be 870. In the light of this the nigh-30-year-old Class '3s' that were banking up to Dalnaspidal in 1948-50 were doing no mean job of work.

After the war the transference of a number of ex-Caledonian 4—4—0s to Highland sheds was made to replace the 'Small Ben' and 'Loch' class 4—4—0s. One of the engines so transferred was Pickersgill 4—4—0 No 14481 (old 76), which had hitherto been moving about among the Glasgow area sheds, thus:

Hamilton	:	Nov 1944 to Oct 1945
Ladyburn	:	Oct 1945 to July 1946
Polmadie	:	July 1946 to July 1947

At the last-named date she was transferred to Inverness, and in January 1948 to Forres. Then on 9 June 1953 she was on the 8.17 pm passenger train from Inverness to Keith, and at Gollanfield Junction came into violent head-on collision with the 5.45 pm freight from Keith to Inverness, hauled by a 'Black Five', No 44783. So far as the Caledonian engine was concerned the affair was an echo of Quintinshill, for she was so badly smashed up that her remains were cut up on the site and removed

to Inverness on 3 July 1953. Fortunately the accident was in itself a fairly minor affair, as related on page 138, but one in which three enginemen were killed and two locomotives destroyed.

As time went on, the Highland line got more and more of the Caledonian superheater 4—4—0s of both McIntosh and Pickersgill types. During 1954, when there were eighteen 'Dunalastair' superheater 'IVs' left, the allocation of these engines was:

Without going into individual allocations the 47 remaining Pickersgills were shedded thus, at midsummer 1954:

Aviemore	3
Balornock	4
Carstairs	5
Dalry Road	1
Dumfries	2
Forfar	1
Forres	4
Helmsdale	2
Hurlford	1
Inverness	4
Ladyburn	7
Motherwell	3
Perth	9
Wick	1

This list does not take account of engines stabled at sub-sheds, such as the Perth engines at Blair Atholl, or Inverness engines at Tain or Fortrose. At that time, including the Perth allocation, there were twenty-eight ex-Caledonian 4—4—0s on the Highland line. They were mostly used on light local passenger work, but those at Perth, sub-shedded at Blair Atholl, and at Aviemore had to assist in working main line trains, both passenger and freight, over the mountains. Those shedded at Dumfries, both McIntosh and Pickersgill, were used almost entirely on freight between that place and Carlisle. For a short time four of the McIntosh engines were at Princes Pier, Greenock, but these four were transferred to Ladyburn by the summer of 1954. Generally speaking, the 'invasion' of Glasgow & South Western territory by these Caledonian superheater 4—4—0s was no more than slight, in the post-war years.

While these working changes were in progress the outward appearance of many individual engines was being changed, and rarely for the better. From the design and performance point of view there was nothing significant about these changes; they were the outcome of a policy of keeping the engines in workable condition at minimum expenditure, and with a gradually contracting range of spare parts.

CR No	BR No	Shed	Age of engine (years)
923	54438	Dumfries	47
924	54439	Inverness	46
139	54440	Ladyburn	44
132	54441	Ladyburn	43
134	54443	Dumfries	43
118	54446	Carstairs	42
120	54448	Perth	42
43	54450	Forfar	41
44	54451	Dalry Road	41
45	54452	Dalry Road	41
46	54453	Ladyburn	41
47	54454	Forfar	41
48	54455	Aviemore	41
39	54456	Ladyburn	40
40	54457	Motherwell	40
41	54458	Inverness	40
42	54459	Wick	40
123	54460	Motherwell	40

THE CALEDONIAN DUNALASTAIRS

It was the fittings rather than the basic essentials that got changed; but of course 'fittings' include such items as chimneys, dome covers, safety valves, and so on. A change in any one of these can alter the whole character of an engine. The Caledonian locomotive stud was, without exception, beautifully proportioned, and the handsomely shaped chimneys and dome covers, whether of the McIntosh or the Pickersgill era, always fitted the general look of the engines to perfection. But take a non-superheated 'Dunalastair II'—one of the most distinctive of them all—put on an *ersatz* Pickersgill chimney, a near-flat-topped dome cover that was much too tall for the chimney, 'pop' safety valves, a raised cab roof, take off the smokebox wings, and put on a six-wheeled tender, and the original designer would hardly recognise the result.

These comments are actually based on a photograph of engine No 776, which as LMSR No 14332 underwent these changes in a 'rebuild', of 1931. At that time, she had also acquired a boiler of the '812' class of 0—6—0. The rebuilding of this engine with a different type of boiler was applied also to engines 767, 773 and 780 of the same class in 1930-3. There had also been the case of 772, which in 1933 underwent a second rebuilding that made her look like a pseudo-Pickersgill—quite a handsome engine. It was only the 'Dunalastair II' engines mentioned that received boilers of different design from the originals. With the changes in appearance of the engines themselves there proceeded also a gradual withdrawal of the bogie tenders. All the 'Dunalastairs' of the second and third series that remained in service received six-wheeled tenders from withdrawn engines of other classes in the 1930s, and a few of the non-superheater 'Dunalastair IVs' were similarly treated. With the superheater engines a number of the McIntosh engines received Pickersgill six-wheeled tenders, and there was a certain amount of interchange of the bogie tenders in that some of the largest ones of the 4,600-galls type became attached to non-superheater 'IVs', and so on. These changes were the result of latter-day expediency, when of course the need for huge tenders had long since disappeared.

To lovers of the old Caledonian Railway and its outstanding pre-grouping character the most depressing change was that of the engine livery. So far as the express passenger 4—4—0s were concerned this underwent five distinct stages from 1923 onwards:

Up goods on Highland line at Kingswood crossing, hauled by Pickersgill 4—4—0 No 54494

One of the last 'Dunalastairs' : No 54458 leaving Inverness on an evening train for the north

1. Midland red, fully lined out in standard Derby style, number in large numerals on tender.
2. Unlined black, but with letters and figures shaded in red, 'L.M.S.' on tenders, numbers on cab sides.
3. Plain black, 'L.M.S.' and numbers in unshaded characters (World War II).
4. First BR style, plain black, numbers in white block letters and BRITISH RAILWAYS in full on tender.
5. BR lined black (LNWR style) with crest on tenders. The first examples of this had BRITISH RAILWAYS in full on the tenders.

Examples of these various styles are shown in the

Two Pickersgills, Nos 54485 and 54486, on the down 'Mail', Perth to Inverness,
leaving Dalwhinnie

133

illustrations, and the impression one forms—entirely in retrospect, however—is that providing the chimneys and dome covers were not too incongruous the effect was not too bad. Considered quite apart from their Caledonian origin, and what had gone before, all the engines covered in this monograph looked splendid in Midland red. The stages of unlined black were depressing, none more so than the earliest BR style with the legend BRITISH RAILWAYS in large white block letters blazoned across tenders which seemed to have something of a matt-black finish. The lined-black style of later days smartened things up considerably, though why the lining on the cab sides should have been finished off only halfway up passes one's comprehension. It looked an unimaginative makeshift, whereas if it had followed the Pickersgill and McIntosh style—and just as easily done—it would have looked infinitely better. Of course there was a degree of cheese-paring in the amount of lining put on. The coupling-rod splashers, the rear coupled wheel splasher, and the forward extension plates of the tender and the footplate doors were not lined at all. On some engines also the running plate valances were not lined. It was nevertheless a relief to have at least a modicum of colour on these engines, and many of them were kept looking reasonably smart right up to the end of their long lives.

A Pickersgill 4—4—0, No 54488, 'stored' in the open at Aviemore, August 1952

CHAPTER 12

ACCIDENTS AND A MAJOR DISASTER

IN a family of engines so long lived as the 'Dunalastairs' and their associates it was inevitable that over the years a number of them should have been involved in accidents, and a chronology of some of the more serious is given herewith. It is nevertheless hard to recall another locomotive family in which no fewer than three were so badly smashed up in collision as to be scrapped outright afterwards. There was the superheater 'IV' No 121 at Quintinshill; a superheater 'III' No 14435 (CR No 900), leading engine of the down 'Royal High-lander' at Dinwoodie in 1928; and finally the Pickersgill 4—4—0 No 14481 (CR No 76) reduced to a tangled mass of steel in the Gollanfield Junction collision in June 1953. Some rather more extended reference is made later to the way in which these three engines and their crews met their deaths.

ACCIDENT CHRONOLOGY : CALEDONIAN RAILWAY

23 Oct 1899	Lambie No 18 ran into a cattle train at Coupar Angus
15 July 1902	'Dunalastair I' No 724, derailed near Bannockburn while on 2 pm ex-Buchanan Street
29 April 1903	'Dunalastair II' No 766 in mishap to 4.25 pm Glasgow to Carlisle
22 Nov 1904	'Dunalastair III' in mishap at Wishaw North Junction
16 Jan 1905	'Dunalastair II' No 774 ran into rear of NBR 5.30 ex-Aberdeen at Craiginches
6 April 1906	'Dunalastair III' No 902 on down 'Corridor' derailed at Kirtlebridge
27 Nov 1908	Down 'Postal' ran into rear of goods at Guthrie: engine No 150 'Dunalastair IV'
19 July 1914	11.20 pm ex-Glasgow (engine 143, 'Dunalastair IV') ran into the rear of
	11.30 pm ex-Waverley at Port Carlisle Junction
29 May 1917	Engines 772, 901, 924, involved in collision between the 9.45 and 10 pm expresses ex-Glasgow at Newton

QUINTINSHILL : 22 MAY 1915

In this, the worst railway accident ever to occur in Great Britain no fewer than five trains were involved. Two were stationary freights, and although both eventually suffered in the terrible fire that raged for nearly twenty-four hours, their engines were undamaged. Of the four engines hauling three passenger trains concerned in the two successive collisions three were 'Dunalastairs'. The prime factor that touched off the whole chain of events was the late running of the midnight sleeping-car express from Euston to Glasgow. There were no doubt extenuating circumstances. It was wartime, and in those early days of the war there was a sustained attempt in certain quarters to preserve a facade of normality. Being the Whitsun weekend there was some extra holiday travel. But having said that, the plain fact remains that if the LNWR had brought the Euston sleeper into Carlisle on time Quintinshill would not have occurred.

Around 6 am on the fatal morning three Caledonian express engines were waiting to go north. One was the big 'Cardean' class 4—6—0 No 907, newly overhauled at St Rollox and being 'run-in' on light duties before taking up her normal heavy express work. She was booked for the 6.10 am 'Parliamentary', a light and relatively unimportant train as far as Beattock; but there it connected with the Tinto express, an outer residential express by which the Caledonian Railway was trying to foster a longer-distance commuter traffic from Glasgow. The connections from roadside stations south of

Beattock were regarded as important, while the engine of the 6.10 from Carlisle transferred to the Tinto at Beattock. As the running of the Tinto was given high priority the 6.10 Carlisle was not a train to be delayed unduly, or sidetracked. It normally followed the Euston sleeper, which was due to leave Carlisle at 6.5 am; but if the latter was running appreciably late it was considered preferable to send the 'Parley' on, and sever the connections from the south to roadside stations on the Caledonian line, rather than risk delaying the Tinto.

The Euston sleeper was one of No 907's regular turns, but while she was 'running-in', a couple of 4—4—0s were substituted, a superheater 'Dunalastair IV', No 48, with a non-superheater 'IV', No 140, as pilot. All these engines were manned by Kingmoor men. That morning the sleeper was wired thirty minutes late, and so the 'Parley' was sent on ahead. Late running at that time was so frequent that a regular operating instruction had been worked out, definitely specifying the procedure to be adopted for varying amounts of lateness of the London train. If it was 'X' minutes late the 'Parley' was to be side-tracked at station 'Y', and so on. By far the most convenient place for the side-tracking was Quintinshill, because there the local could be run direct into the loop line on the down side, and no actual shunting was needed. That morning, however, the down loop was occupied by a freight train, and so the only way to clear the down main line for the 6.5 am express was to shunt the 'Parley' back over the trailing crossover on to the up main line.

How the signalman at Quintinshill carried out this manoeuvre, and then proceeded to forget all about the standing local train is a tragic and well-known story; and having placed a mighty obstruction on the up main line, in the shape of the 'Cardean' class 4—6—0 No 907, the 'Dunalastairs' enter the story. An up troop special from Larbert, conveying men of the 1/7th Battalion of the Royal Scots, en route for Gallipoli, was accepted and all signals lowered for it to pass—even though the line was blocked, not at some unseen spot but just outside the signal box! It was a heavy train of twenty-one vehicles consisting of four GCR bogie coaches; eleven GCR six-wheelers; five Caledonian six-wheeled vans, and an open bogie scenery truck. It was hauled by one of the Kingmoor 'Dunalastair IV' superheaters, No 121, manned by her regular crew, Driver F. Scott and Fireman J. Hannah. Running under clear signals, and on a falling gradient of 1 in 200, it came on at about 70 mph. The line south of Kirkpatrick is quite straight for about three miles, but just as Quintinshill is approached there is a right-

hand curve on a radius of eighty chains. At the very commencement of the curve there is an overbridge.

Travelling south on the footplate, Quintinshill box can be seen through the overbridge for some considerable time, but the slight curve and the presence of another train in the down loop on that fatal morning no doubt obscured the view of the standing train, and it was only when they were too close to do much about it that Scott and Hannah saw the massive front of No 907 right in their path. When two such engines meet in head-on collision, at a speed probably at least of 50 mph, the impact is terrible, and both engines were wrecked beyond repair. The 'Dunalastair IV' suffered more severely than the 4—6—0, and after she was finally extricated from beneath the burnt-out ruins of her train it was decided to scrap her forthwith. It was hoped to save No 907, and she was towed back to St Rollox. She lay there for some time before it was finally decided that she was beyond repair. After the first collision her huge bogie tender lay right across the down main line. All signals were off for the 6.5 express, and although these were put back when the signalman realised his terrible error it was too late, and engines 140 and 48 came storming up from Gretna at 60 mph, ploughed through the scattered wreckage of the troop train, much of which had shot clean over the top of engines 121 and 907, and then crashed into 907's tender.

This great 57-ton obstruction was driven forward amongst the wagons of the standing goods train, to involve them in the ensuing fire; but the 6.5 am express was not like the troop train. It was composed of thirteen vehicles of heavy modern WCJS corridor stock, and in bringing it to a violent stop from a speed of 60 mph the engines were driven forward and the first three coaches telescoped. Despite all this, however, the robust construction of the engines and their tenders not only enabled them to survive the impact, and emerge so little damaged that they could be repaired and run for many years subsequently, but all four enginemen survived. It was indeed only the driver of the leading engine who was at all seriously injured. Engine No 140 put in another twenty-six years of service, while No 48, as British Railways No 54455, was not withdrawn until July 1954.

As a tailpiece to this dreadful affair it can be added that Frank Scott's widow received £300 compensation from the company, and £10 annually for her two youngest children until they were sixteen. Fireman Hannah's widow received three years' earnings, equal to £270 5s 9d, plus £10 per annum for five years for her five-year-old boy.

DINWOODIE: 25 OCTOBER 1928

The second 'Dunalastair' to be scrapped as a result of a collision was also the victim of a signalman's error. This time it was the once-celebrated 'Tourist' express, though by 1928 officially named 'The Royal Highlander' by the LMSR. As in the earliest days of the 'Dunalastairs' it ran non-stop from Carlisle to Stirling, though it was not quite the prestige job for the locomotive department that it was in former days. All fifty of the 'Royal Scot' engines were then in service, but none were available for this train, and as in Caledonian days the working formed a 'double-home' turn for engines and men between Carlisle and Aberdeen, but by then using Midland compounds. The train was a heavy one, conveying sleeping-car portions from Euston to both Aberdeen and Inverness, and although the Scottish traffic had eased off a good deal by that time of year the train consisted nevertheless of twelve vehicles, with a tare weight of 347 tons, and the compound 1176 was double-headed from Carlisle by 'Dunalastair III' No 14435, old No 900, which had been superheated since 1918, and was LMSR Class '3'. They left Carlisle about four minutes late.

Ahead of them was a regular freight train which was booked to shunt for them at Beattock. It was worked by one of the Pickersgill '60' class 4—6—0s built after grouping, and which therefore never had Caledonian numbers. This engine was evidently not in the best of condition, and on the previous night the driver had trouble with one of the left-hand coupling rod pins. On the night of the accident he heard a rattling noise just after passing through Dinwoodie, thought it was the same trouble again, and stopped the train for examination, with the rear brakevan about 700 yards north of the Dinwoodie starting signal, and three-quarters of a mile beyond the signalbox. On examination he found that the coupling rod of the mechanical lubricator had become detached, and he proceeded to make the necessary repair. The guard unfortunately did not take very prompt measures to protect the temporarily stranded train. He went forward, examining the wagons in turn, and apparently spent some time talking to the driver, and watching him do the repair. It was only when he realised the 'Royal Highlander' was due that he hurried back to his van, and took steps to place some detonators on the line.

Of course he was justified in expecting that the express, if it approached, would have been stopped by signal at Dinwoodie, but that did not excuse his dilatoriness in protecting his train. As it was, a shocking blunder in the block working had been committed by the signalman in the next box ahead, Wamphray. After having accepted the goods, had it accepted by the box ahead, and pulled off his signals he dozed off, and was awakened by the Dinwoodie man enquiring about 'line clear' for the express. Looking at the clock and assuming that the goods must have passed while he was asleep, he quite erroneously cleared his instrument, and accepted the express. The Dinwoodie man was a little mystified that the goods had taken so long to 'clear' the section, whereas in fact it was still stationary only three-quarters of a mile beyond his box. At 3 am, however, it was pitch dark, and although the line is straight it would not have been possible to see a red tail lamp at that distance. So despite a slight suspicion in his mind that something was not quite in order, he cleared all his signals for the express.

The stretch of line just north of Lockerbie usually witnessed the fastest running south of Beattock Summit by a northbound train, and the two engines of the 'Royal Highlander' were going hard, at well over 60 mph. They passed Dinwoodie under clear signals, and by the time the leading driver saw the red tail lamp of the goods there was time to do little more than close the regulator. They collided with the goods virtually at full speed. At that spot the line is on a shallow embankment, and No 14435 after ploughing through and completely destroying fourteen wagons went down the bank and turned over on her left side. The compound followed her, but slid right over the top of the 'Dunalastair', and finished about an engine's length *ahead*. The tender of No 1176 jack-knifed with the engine and ended up almost at right-angles to the track on top of No 14435, while the leading van of the express remained coupled to the tender with its leading bogie high in the air, and precariously above No 14435.

In this most violent collision all four enginemen of the express were killed, though no other persons were injured at all. Modern coaching stock, and the presence of the two vans next to the engines saved the day.

The framing and machinery of No 14435 was smashed beyond repair, and she was subsequently scrapped; but the boiler was no more than slightly damaged. It was repaired and allocated in 1930 to a non-superheated member of the same class, No 14347 (Old 897). This latter engine thereupon became superheated, and was upgraded to Class '3'. As such she ran for another nine years.

THE CALEDONIAN DUNALASTAIRS

GOLLANFIELD: 9 JUNE 1953

The summer timetable for Coronation year came into force on 8 June, and in it a new evening train from Inverness to Keith was put on, leaving the former place at 8.17 pm. As is often the case with a new service its existence was at first little known, and it was poorly patronised. In the circumstances it was very fortunate that this was so. In fact there were only three passengers in the four coaches forming this train. The engine was Pickersgill 4—4—0 No 54481 (CR No 76). Double line then existed from Inverness to Dalcross, but from the latter point eastwards the line was single, equipped with electric tablet instruments, with apparatus for mechanical token exchange. At that time, the former LMSR regulations for single line working were in force.

Travelling westwards was the 5.45 pm unfitted freight train from Keith to Inverness. This train had a very ample time schedule, presumably to provide margin for shunting at many intermediate points. It was not booked to leave Forres till 9.10 pm—a time of 3 h 25 m for a distance of only $30\frac{1}{4}$ miles from Keith; but evidently no more traffic was awaiting it, or expected, and the actual departure from Forres was at 7.55 pm. Although the train was thus running so much ahead of time the driver seemed to be in a hurry, and with a Stanier Class '5' 4—6—0 and only nineteen wagons and a 20-ton brake van he ran fast to Nairn. There a further twenty wagons were attached, and despite the marshalling involved the train was ready to leave only twenty-five minutes after leaving Forres, $9\frac{1}{2}$ miles away. The signalman at Nairn was a little hesitant to allow the train to leave, as there seemed a possibility of delaying the 8.17 pm eastbound stopping train from Inverness, which would have to be crossed at Gollanfield Junction, $5\frac{1}{2}$ miles. But the driver of the goods assured the signalman at Nairn that he would get to Gollanfield in ten minutes, and so, after advising the latter signalman, the goods was allowed to leave Nairn at 8.22 pm.

At that time of year it was of course broad daylight in those latitudes, and although cloudy the visibility was good. Hauling now a load of forty vehicles the Stanier 4—6—0 continued to be driven exceptionally fast for an unfitted goods train, especially considering that the train was already so far ahead of time. The regulations prescribed that: 'when trains which have to cross each other are approaching a token station in opposite directions, the signals in both directions must be kept at

danger and when the train which has first to be allowed to draw forward has been brought to a stand, the home signal applicable to such train may be taken off to allow it to draw forward to the station or to the starting signal and after it has again come to a stand and the signalman has ascertained that the line on which the other train will arrive is clear, the necessary signals for that train may be taken off'.

On the other hand, the LNER regulations which had operated on the GNSR line until nationalisation permitted the home signal to be lowered when the signalman judged the train first to arrive in a crossing loop had come *nearly* to a stand.

When looking down a line towards an oncoming train it is sometimes difficult to judge the speed. But the signalman at Gollanfield made a serious misjudgment when the goods was approaching, and he lowered his home signal prematurely. It may have misled the driver, although from the conversation with the signalman at Nairn he must have known he had to cross the 8.17 pm passenger train at Gollanfield. Whether he was misled or not, Colonel McMullen, who conducted the subsequent enquiry, considered that the driver had set up the conditions for an accident by approaching the distant signal at a speed that could not have been less than 55 mph, requiring a stopping distance of 2,300 yd even with full brake power. This would have caused the train to overshoot the facing points at the west end of the loop by some 500 yd.

All the evidence went to show that the driver made no more than a slight application of the brakes, and witnesses on the station could not recollect that there was any clanging of buffers among the loose-coupled wagons. In the meantime the 8.17 pm from Inverness, hauled by the Pickersgill 4—4—0 No 54481, was running slowly up to the home signal, preparing to stop, and doing not more than 20 mph. Then its enginemen were doubtless horrified to see the freight come careering through the station at fully 45 mph. They remained at their posts, and must have been killed instantly in the frightful collision that followed. As the official report stated, the engine became a tangled mass of metal, and the Stanier engine also was wrecked beyond repair. The combined speed of the two trains can have been little less than 70 mph, and so far as damage to engines was concerned Quintinshill was no more than a 'bump-up' compared to this apocalyptic smash on the heathlands beside the Moray Firth. So ended the Pickersgill 4—4—0 No 54481.

A Pickersgill, No 54471, at Achnasheen, Dingwall & Skye line

PICKERSGILLS IN THE HIGHLANDS

A Pickersgill, No 14467, on down goods at Ballinling

CASE HISTORIES

1.   THE 'DUNALASTAIR I' CLASS

Built at St Rollox to Order Number Y44

CR No	Date built	First shed	First driver	LMSR No	Date scrapped
721	28.1.96	Polmadie	J. Ranochan	14311	—/31
722	7.2.96	Perth	W. Hamilton	14312	11/33
723	14.2.96	Perth	A. Brown	14313	8/33
724	20.2.96	Perth	J. Soutar	14314	—/30
725	27.2.96	Perth	J. Mitchell	14315	10/35
726	9.3.96	Aberdeen	H. Brown	14316	—/35
727	18.3.96	Carlisle	T. Armstrong	14317	—/32
728	30.3.96	Carlisle	T. Tervitt	14318	12/34
729	3.4.96	Carlisle	A. Crooks	14319	—/32
730	9.4.96	Carlisle	B. Johnston	14320	—/31
731	16.4.96	Dalry Road	J. Dick	14321	—/31
732	23.4.96	Carlisle	W. Lawson	14322	12/33
733	30.4.96	Carlisle	T. Robinson	14323	—/32
734	7.5.96	Polmadie	A. Dunn	14324	—/30
735	14.5.96	Polmadie	J. Bain	14325	—/33

721 named *Dunalastair*
723 named *Victoria*
724 named *Jubilee*

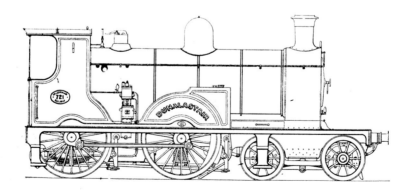

2. THE REBUILT DRUMMONDS

WITH 'DUNALASTAIR I' BOILER

Original No	Built			Renumbered				Scrapped
	Date	Works	Rebuilt St Rollox	No	Date		LMSR No	
66	1884	Neilsons	Mar 1901	1066	Oct 1922		14298	Jan 1930
70	1884	,,	April 1901	1070	Nov 1922		14299 §	— 1927
71	1884	,,	July 1898	1071	Nov 1922		14300 §	— 1927
73	1884	,,	Feb 1902	1073	April 1920		14301	— 1928
75	1884	,,	May 1901	1075	June 1920		14302	Oct 1929
60	1885	St Rollox	Dec 1901	1060*	Mar 1916		14303 §	Oct 1929
62	1885	,,	April 1902	1062†	Mar 1916		14304	— 1931
63	1885	,,	April 1902	1063	1916		—	Nov 1916
64	1885	,,	Dec 1901	1064	Jan 1917		—	May 1921
65	1885	,,	June 1901	1065	Jan 1917		—	May 1917

* Renumbered 17 in Nov 1916 : 1060 again in 1922
† Renumbered 87 in Nov 1916 : 1062 again in 1921
§ LMSR number allocated, but engine never repainted
and renumbered

A rebuilt Drummond, No 1066, on Arbroath - Perth stopping train near Luncarty

3. THE 'DUNALASTAIR II' CLASS

Built at St Rollox to Order Number Y51

CR No	Date built	Date rebuilt*	Nature of rebuild	LMSR No	Date scrapped
766	18.12.97	10/14	Superheated	14430	1/36
767	28.12.97	1933	'812' class boiler	14326	—/39
768	26.1.98	—		14327	8/36
769	26.1.98	1/15	Superheated	14431	2/36
770	4.2.98	—		14328	—/40
771	18.2.98	3/14	Superheated	14432	3/35
772	1.2.98	7/14†	Superheated	14433	3/36
773	18.2.98	1930	'812' class boiler	14329	12/36
774	24.2.98	—		14330	—/41
775	9.3.98	—		14331	—/45
776	16.3.98	1931	'812' class boiler	14332	—/46
777	25.3.98	—		14333	9/47
778	31.3.98	—		14334	
779	6.4.98	—		14335	—/39
780	18.4.98	1933	'812' class boiler	14336	5/39

766 was named *Dunalastair 2nd*
779 was named *Bredalbane*

* All engines of this class were rebuilt at some time during their lives; but dates are given only in the case of those equipped with superheaters, or different types of boilers. Those rebuilt with '812' class boilers remained saturated.

† Rebuilt a second time in 1933, with Pickersgill 0—6—0 superheater boiler.

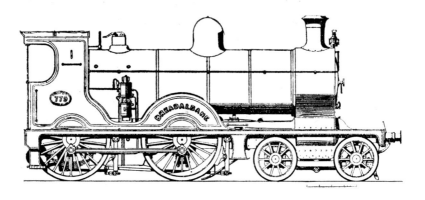

4. THE 'DUNALASTAIR III' CLASS

| | Built at St Rollox | | Order Number Y57 for engines 900-902 | | | |
| | | | „   „   Y62 „   „   887-899 | | | |

CR No	Date built	Date rebuilt		LMSR No	Date scrapped
900	13.12.99	5/18	Superheated	14435	10/28*
901	21.12.99	3/14	Superheated	14436	11/37
902	4.12.99			14346	—/39
887	27.4.00			14337	4/47
888	9.5.00			14338	3/46
889	21.5.00			14339	—/41
890	4.6.00			14340	12/46
891	19.6.00			14341	6/39
892	2.7.00			14342	3/39
893	6.7.00			14343	—/32
894	26.6.00	4/16	Superheated	14434	4/48
895	13.6.00			14344	—/49
896	30.5.00			14345	—/41
897	14.5.00	—/30†	Superheated	14347	—/39
898	4.5.00	7/14	Superheated	14437	—/39
899	25.4.00	1/23	Superheated	14348	—/44

The Caledonian numbering of the engines on order number Y62 was not in date order, but the LMSR numbering followed sequentially on the CR number for the non-superheated engines.

* Scrapped as a result of extensive damage sustained in the Dinwoodie accident, when No 14435 was leading engine of the down 'Royal Highlander' when it collided with a stationary goods train.

† Received boiler off the scrapped 14435; fitted with piston valves and up-graded to LMS Class '3'.

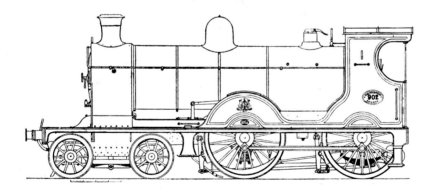

5. THE 'DUNALASTAIR IV' CLASS

Built at St Rollox

ORDER No Y72

CR No	Date built	LMSR No	Date scrapped
140	21.5.04	14349	—/41
141	31.5.04	14350	10/45
142	9.6.04	14351	—/39
143	17.6.04	14352	4/37
144	24.6.04	14353	—/37

ORDER No Y76

CR No	Date built	LMSR No	Date scrapped
145	30.11.05	14354	—/42
146	12.12.05	14355	4/39
147★	19.12.05	14356	—/41
148	21.12.05	14357	8/38
149	29.12.05	14358	—/40
150	12.1.06	14359	9/38

ORDER No Y85

CR No	Date built	LMSR No	Date scrapped
923†	24.12.07	14438	5/55
924†	13.1.08	14439	8/58
925	23.1.08	14360	12/43
926	29.1.08	14361	3/37
927	1.2.08	14362	3/37

ORDER No Y92

CR No	Date built	LMSR No	Date scrapped
136	6.7.10	14365	4/39
137	20.6.10	14363	10/48
138	5.7.10	14364	2/39
139§	7.10	14440	1/57

★ Superheated, retaining slide valves in 12/22
† Superheated, with piston valves : 924 in 5/15, and 925 in 5/19
§ Built new as superheater, with piston valves

6. THE SUPERHEATER 'DUNALASTAIR IVs'

Built at St Rollox

CR No	Date built	LMSR No	BR No and date		Date scrapped
132	11.4.11	14441	54441	3/50	5/59
133	24.4.11	14442	—	—	7/46
134	2.5.11	14443	54443	4/48	10/55
135	13.5.11	14444	54444	4/48	10/53
117	—/12	14445	54445	5/48	10/52
118	—/12	14446	54446	9/48	8/55
119	—/12	14447	54447	7/50	6/53
120	—/12	14448	54448	8/48	3/55
121*	—/12	—	—	—	11/15
122	—/13	14449	54449	6/50	11/53
43	—/13	14450	54450	12/49	10/55
44	—/13	14451	54451	10/49	9/55
45	—/13	14452	54452	6/49	7/57
46	—/13	14453	54453	9/48	8/57
47	—/13	14454	54454	11/51	10/55
48	—/13	14455	54455	5/48	7/54
39	23.5.14	14456	54456	3/49	2/57
40	11.5.14	14457	54457	11/48	2/55
41	27.4.14	14458	54458	12/48	2/57
42	17.4.14	14459	54459	4/49	12/54
123	2.5.14	14460	54460	—/49	10/55

* Damaged beyond repair at Quintinshill

This class also included engines 923, 924 and 139 (LMSR 14438, 14439 and 14440) originally built to the 'Dunalastair IV' non-superheater orders.

K

7.   THE PICKERSGILL 4—4—0s

CR Number	Builder	Order No or Maker's No	Date built	LMSR No	Renumbered by BR	Date scrapped
113	CR St Rollox	Y 113	5/16	14461	9/50	5/59
114	,,	,,	-/16	14462	11/48	5/60
115	,,	,,	-/16	14463	6/48	12/62
116	,,	,,	-/16	14464	7/48	10/61
121	,,	,,	-/16	14465	9/48	10/62
124	,,	,,	-/16	14466	7/48	3/62
928	NB Loco Atlas	21442	-/16	14467	2/51	10/61
929	,,	21443	-/16	14468	1/50	10/59
930	,,	21444	-/16	14469	1/49	11/59
931	,,	21445	-/16	14470	9/48	12/59
932	,,	21446	-/16	14471	5/48	10/59
933	,,	21447	-/16	14472	11/49	10/59
934	,,	21448	-/16	14473	8/48	10/59
935	,,	21449	-/16	14474	11/48	10/59
936	,,	21450	-/16	14475	4/49	6/61
937	,,	21451	-/16	14476	10/50	3/60
72	CR St Rollox	Y 124	5/20	14477	4/49	5/60
73	,,	,,	5/20	14478	2/49	7/61
74	,,	,,	6/20	14479	5/48	10/59
75	,,	,,	7/20	14480	10/48	8/60
76	,,	,,	7/20	14481	2/49	6/53★
77	,,	,,	7/20	14482	6/50	3/62
78	,,	,,	8/20	14483	10/49	6/61
79	,,	,,	9/20	14484	9/48	11/59
80	,,	,,	9/20	14485	5/48	10/61
81	,,	,,	9/20	14486	6/50	3/62
82	Armstrong Whitworth	111	2/21	14487	2/51	3/61
83	,,	112	3/21	14488	7/48	2/61
84	,,	113	3/21	14489	4/50	12/61
85	,,	114	4/21	14490	6/49	5/60
86	,,	115	4/21	14491	6/48	12/61
87	,,	116	4/21	14492	4/49	11/61
88	,,	117	5/21	14493	2/50	11/61
89	,,	118	5/21	14494	9/50	8/60
90	,,	119	6/21	14495	12/49	3/62
91	,,	120	6/21	14496	10/48	10/59
66	NB Loco Hyde Park	22943	11/22	14497	10/48	10/59
67	,,	22944	,,	14498	6/49	5/60
68	,,	22945	,,	14499	5/48	5/60
69	,,	22946	12/22	14500	12/49	3/62
70	,,	22947	,,	14501	12/49	12/61
71	,,	22948	,,	14502	4/49	10/62
92	,,	22949	,,	14503	10/49	10/59
93	,,	22950	,,	14504	3/49	10/59
94	,,	22951	,,	14505	10/48	4/61
95	,,	22952	,,	14506	7/48	11/61
96	,,	22953	,,	14507	1/50	11/61
97	,,	22954	,,	14508	1/49	12/59

★ Scrapped on site after the Gollanfield collision of 9 June 1953

Pickersgill 4—4—0 No 114: one of the first batch, built at St Rollox in 1916

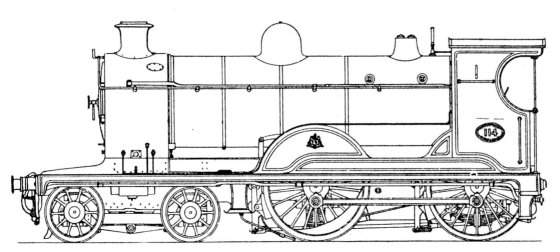

An interesting 'Dunalastair' derivative : one of the '34' class of 2—6—0 superheated mixed traffic engines built 1912 at St Rollox

APPENDIX I

ALLOCATION OF CALEDONIAN 4—4—0s AT MIDSUMMER 1945

Aviemore:	14338 (non-super'd 'III')
	14434 (super'd 'III')
Balornock:	14473/74/75/83/87/94 (all Pickersgills)
Carstairs:	14350 (non-super'd 'IV')
	14438/39/46/49 (super'd 'IV')
	14463/70/71/72/77/80/84/90 and 14505 (Pickersgill)
Corkerhill:	14363 (non-super'd 'IV')
Dalry Road:	14442/51/52 (super'd 'IV')
	14478, 14507 (Pickersgill)
Forfar:	14450/54 (super'd 'IV')
	14486 (Pickersgill)
Forres:	14333 (non-super'd 'II')
	14337 (non-super'd 'III')
Hamilton:	14481 (Pickersgill)
Hurlford:	14495, 14504 (Pickersgill)
Inverness:	14332 (non-super'd 'II')
	14340 (non-super'd 'III')
Ladyburn:	14440/43/44/45/57 (super'd 'IV')
	14461/68/79/92/97 and 14508 (Pickersgill)
Motherwell:	14460 (super'd 'IV')
	14462/64/65/98 and 14506 (Pickersgill)
Perth:	14447/48/58 (super'd 'IV')
	14467/69/76/82/89/93/99 and 14500/1/2/3 (Pickersgill)
Polmadie:	14441/53/56/59 (super'd 'IV')
	14488 (Pickersgill)
Stirling:	14455 (super'd 'IV')
	14466/85/91/96 (Pickersgill)

APPENDIX 2

CALEDONIAN 4—4—0s : DIMENSIONS

Class	Lambie	'Dun I'	'Dun II'	'Dun III'	'Dun IV' '140' class	'Dun IV' '117' class Superh'd	P'kersgill
Nominal tractive effort at 85% boiler pressure . . . . . lb.	14,640	15,100	17,900	18,411	18,411	19,751	21,432
Cylinders:							
Diameter and stroke in	19 x 26	$19\frac{1}{4}$ x 26	19 x 26	19 x 26	19 x 26	$20\frac{1}{4}$ x 26	$20\frac{1}{2}$ x 26
Distance, centre to centre ft in	2—3	2—3	$2—4\frac{1}{2}$	$2—4\frac{1}{2}$	$2—4\frac{1}{2}$	$2—4\frac{1}{2}$	$2—1\frac{1}{2}$
Valves	Slide	Slide	Slide	Slide	Slide	Piston	Piston
Valve gear	Steph'son	Steph'son	Steph'son	Steph'son	Steph'son	Steph'son	Steph'son
Connecting rods, length ft in	6—6	6—6	7—1	7—1	7—1	7—1	7—1
Wheels:							
Driving and coupled wheels dia ft in	6—6	6—6	6—6	6—6	6—6	6—6	6—6
Bogie dia ft in	3—6	3—6	3—6	3—6	3—6	3—6	3—6
Wheelbases:							
Centre of bogies to centre of driving axle ft in	9—11	9—11	10—11	10—11	10—11	10—11	11—2
Centre to centre bogie wheels ft in	6—6	6—6	6—6	6—6	6—6	6—6	7—0
Centre of driving to centre of trailing axle ft in	9—0	9—0	9—0	9—6	9—9	9—9	9—9
Total wheelbase, engine ft in	22—1	22—1	23—1	23—7	23—10	23—10	24—4
Total wheelbase, engine and tender ft in	$44—5\frac{1}{2}$	$44—5\frac{1}{2}$	$49—2\frac{1}{2}$	$49—2\frac{1}{2}$	$49—2\frac{1}{2}$	$49—5\frac{1}{2}$	$46—8\frac{1}{2}$
Total length over buffers ft in	$53—9\frac{3}{4}$	$53—9\frac{3}{4}$	$57—3\frac{3}{4}$	$57—3\frac{3}{4}$	58—2	58—2	56—2
Boiler and firebox:							
Diameter of barrel, mean outside ft in	$4—6\frac{1}{4}$	$4—9\frac{1}{4}$	$4—9\frac{1}{4}$	$4—9\frac{1}{4}$	$4—11\frac{1}{2}$	$4—11\frac{1}{2}$	$4—11\frac{1}{2}$
Length of barrel ft in	$10—3\frac{1}{2}$	$10—3\frac{1}{2}$	11—1	11—1	11—2	11—2	11—2
Height to centre from rail ft in	7—3	7—9	7—9	8—0	8—3	8—3	8—3
Steam pressure lb per sq in	160	160	175	180	180	170	180
Tubes:							
Material	Brass	Brass	Copper	Copper	Copper	Steel	Steel
Number, small	238	265	265	269	276	163	157
Number, large	—	—	—	—	—	24	24
Length between tube plates ft in	10—7	10—7	$11—4\frac{1}{2}$	$11—4\frac{1}{2}$	11—6	11—6	11—6
Heating surface:							
Tubes, small sq ft	1 071·5	1,284·45	1,381·22	1,402	1,470	1,220	827
Tubes, large sq ft	—	—	—	—	—	295	358
Firebox sq ft	112·62	118·78	118·78	138	145	145	144
Total sq ft	1,184·12	1,403·23	1,500·0	1,540	1,615	1,365	1,329
Superheater sq ft	—	—	—	—	—	295	200
Total equivalent sq ft	—	—	—	—	—	1,660	1,529
Grate area sq ft	19·5	20·63	20·63	22	21	21	20·7
Weights on bogie tons	14·66	15·7	16·3	17·05	18·75	21	21·5
Driving axle tons	15·35	16·0	16·85	17·5	{37·75	{38	19·9
Trailing axle tons	15·2	15·25	15·85	17·1			19·85
Total weight, engine tons	45·25	46·95	49·0	51·65	56·5	59	61·25
Tender:							
Wheels dia ft in	3—6	3—6	3—6	3—6	3—6	3—6	4—0
Wheelbase ft in	13—0	16—9	16—6	16—6	16—6	16—6	13—0
Capacity of tanks gals	3,570	4,125	4,125	4,125	4,300	4,600	4,200
Coal capacity tons	$4\frac{1}{2}$	$4\frac{1}{2}$	$4\frac{1}{2}$	$4\frac{1}{2}$	$4\frac{1}{2}$	6	6
Weight loaded tons	39·05	45	45	$49\frac{1}{2}$	56	56	$46\frac{1}{2}$
Total weight engine and tender in working order tons	84·3	94	96·7	101·2	112·5	115	109
Ratios:							
Weight on coupled axles / Tractive power	4·68	4·63	4·08	4·22	4·6	4·3	4·16
Total engine weight / Equivalent heating surface	85·7	75·0	73·3	75·2	78·7	79·7	84·0
Tractive power x dia of drivers / Equivalent heating surface	967	838	930	930	888	927	1,092
Tractive power / Grate area	750	729	865	838	873	939	1,036
Equivalent heating surface / Grate area	60·8	67·8	72·4	69·8	76·3	79·0	73·8

APPENDIX 3

A NOTE ON THE 'GOUROCK FLYERS'

THE use of the 'Dunalastairs' on the Gourock trains raises an interesting point in the history of locomotive working in Scotland. In Drummond's day, in view of his particular association with the district, one would naturally expect that special attention would be given to the provision of motive power for the Clyde coast services, and sure enough he built what could be termed a 'mixed traffic' version of his main-line express passenger 4—4—0s specially for the job. The 'Greenock Bogies', as they became known, were, however, a generally smaller engine than the 6 ft 6 in main-line 'greyhounds'. The boilers had a total heating surface of $936\frac{1}{2}$ sq ft, against 1,208 sq ft; the cylinders were 18 in diameter by 26 in stroke, as on the main-line engines; and the coupled wheels were 5 ft 9 in diameter. At the time these engines were built, however, in 1887 the Gourock extension had not been built, and competition with the Glasgow & South Western, although keen, had not risen to the degree of fever heat that it attained by the turn of the century.

On the 'Sou' West', Hugh Smellie also introduced a special class for the Clyde services, the celebrated 'Wee Bogies', the basic dimensions of which were very similar to those of their Caledonian rivals, and were, in their turn, generally smaller than the 'Pullman' engines. The Sou' West had much more reason to use smaller-wheeled engines on its Clyde coast run, for the gradients between Paisley and Greenock were very severe. When Smellie came over to the Caledonian it is interesting to speculate whether he would have persisted with small-wheeled 4—4—0s in view of the speeds required by the fastest Gourock trains. Although not all the boat trains were timed so sharply as the 4.8 pm out of 'Central' the whole service was extremely smart. On paper the allowance of only 32 min for the 26 miles from 'Central' to Gourock does look venturesome, against the background of the period; but since the line has been electrified I have had the opportunity of riding over it in the cabs of some of the fast trains, and it does not appear so difficult as has sometimes been made out.

Although the start out of Glasgow Central requires slow running until the direct line from the south is joined at Shields there is then a fine straight stretch almost to Paisley. It is true there is a heavy speed restriction for the junction and curves through Gilmour Street, but after that fast time can be made to the outskirts of Port Glasgow. On a recent trip I clocked 8.1 miles from Paisley St James to Langbank to be covered in 7 min without exceeding 73 mph. With the 'Dunalastairs' in the form they were displaying on the 'Tourist' express, and elsewhere there should have been no difficulty in passing Port Glasgow, 20.3 miles from 'Central', in about 23 min, and this would have left a comfortable 9 min for the last six sharply-curved miles into Gourock.

Rous-Marten, writing in February 1898 after some footplate runs on the 'Dunalastair II' class engines, reported: 'The third trial'—after some on the Carlisle road—'was on a smaller scale. It was made with the second of the new engines, No 767, on the fast boat train known as the Gourock express, which leaves Glasgow at 4.13 p.m., and is timed to run to Gourock, $26\frac{1}{4}$ miles, in 35 minutes over a road somewhat heavy in parts, and remarkable for its continuity of exceedingly sharp curves. The load in this case amounted to about 200 tons. There was no opportunity of testing the quickest time in which the run could be made, because under an arrangement with the Glasgow and South-Western Railway this train is not permitted to arrive at Gourock much under the prescribed time. However, by making a somewhat deliberate start and not indulging in any hurry until after Paisley was passed, the engine was able to display some fast running, attaining a speed of 76.3 m.p.h., and running to Gourock in 31 min. 44 sec. from Glasgow.'

Euston - Glasgow express leaving Carlisle with engines 926 'Dunalastair IV' and 1073
(rebuilt Drummond)

Down West Coast express leaving Carlisle, hauled by the pioneer 'Dunalastair III' No 902

APPENDIX 4

PAINTING OF CALEDONIAN EXPRESS PASSENGER LOCOMOTIVES

The beauty of the Caledonian style of passenger engine painting is one of those features of the pre-grouping scene on British railways that have become almost legendary: 'Caley Blue'—what memories it conjures up!

The actual shade of blue varied over the years. The first, second and third series of 'Dunalastairs' originally had the dark and very dignified Prussian blue of Victorian times. So far as 4—4—0 engines were concerned the lighter shade, an almost ethereal sky blue, came in with the 'Dunalastair IV' class though this was subject to variations in shade, particularly when engines like the Pickersgill 4—4—0s included batches built by outside contractors. Just before grouping a number of engines were running in a distinctly darker shade of blue.

Apart from the blue, the basic colour scheme included crimson lake for the running plate valances, the steps, and the tender underframes, and vermilion for the buffer beams of both engine and tender. The vermilion panel was restricted, however, to the space between the buffers. The outer flanks, and the buffer shanks were crimson lake. The wheels were blue with black tyres, and the engine underframes black. Other main features were:

1. Initials C.R. and engine number on the front beam.
2. The engine number was displayed on the back of the tender tank.
3. The coat of arms was displayed on the leading coupled wheel splashers, and also between the initials C R on the tenders. An exception to this was the 'Dunalastair I' class when first built, which had a single full-stop between the initials C.R.
4. An interesting point was that the back cab-roof angle face was painted red.
5. The lettering on the tenders, and on the splashers of those engines that were named was gilt, shaded on the left in red with white highlights.
6. The number plates fixed to the cab-sides were of cast brass, and included the railway company's name, the number, and the building date. When this type superseded the flat engraved brass plates of the Drummond era the background to the raised letters and figures was red; but it was later changed to engine-blue.
7. The lining-out consisted of black bands edged on both sides with a white line. Various photographs in this book show clearly the style of the lining, and this was used also on the Westinghouse brake pump. The edging of the crimson parts was black, with a white line dividing the lake and the black.
8. The tender axle-boxes and springs were black, though there was a small panel on the lids of the axle-boxes which was painted lake, edged with white. Although it is no part of the 'Dunalastair' story, I can add that the outside cylinder engines of the Pickersgill era had lake cylinder covers, lined with black having white edgings.
9. The safety valve casing levers were red.

APPENDIX 5

'DUNALASTAIR' CHRONOLOGY

	1895	John Farquharson McIntosh appointed locomotive superintendent
January	1896	First 'Dunalastair' No 721 built
December	1897	First 'Dunalastair II' 4—4—0 built
February	1898	Belgian Government requests supply of five 'Dunalastair II' engines
December	1899	First 'Dunalastair III' 4—4—0 built
May	1904	First 'Dunalastair IV' 4—4—0 built
July	1910	First superheater 4—4—0 built, No 139
April	1911	Superheater 'Dunalastair IV' class commenced
	1914	William Pickersgill, locomotive superintendent
May	1915	Quintinshill disaster: engine 121 destroyed
May	1916	First Pickersgill 4—4—0 built
December	1922	Last Pickersgill 4—4—0 built
January	1923	Caledonian Rly became part of the LMSR
December	1924	Engine No 124 tested between Carlisle and Leeds
October	1928	Superheater 'Dunalastair III' No 14435 scrapped after the Dinwoodie accident
—	1930	First 'Dunalastair I' class scrapped
March	1935	First 'Dunalastair II' class scrapped
October	1935	Last 'Dunalastair I' class scrapped
March	1937	First 'Dunalastair IV' class scrapped
—	1949	Last non-superheater 4—4—0 scrapped
June	1953	Gollanfield Junc collision, Pickersgill 4—4—0 No 54481 scrapped
May	1959	Last 'Dunalastair IV' superheater No 54441 scrapped
December	1962	Last Pickersgill 4—4—0 (54463) scrapped

APPENDIX 6

THE 'DUNALASTAIR' INFLUENCE

THERE is little doubt that the original 'Dunalastair' of 1896 was one of the most outstanding engines of its day. The impact of its success on locomotive practice in many parts of the world was tremendous. In Belgium in particular the 'Dunalastair' influence went far beyond the purchase of five of the second, or '766' class. Many more up to a total of 230 of a slightly enlarged design were built in Belgium, and the general McIntosh style and detail design were embodied in 0—6—0 goods and 4—4—2 passenger tank engines for the Belgian State Railway. A beautiful model of one of the Belgian-built 4—4—0 express engines is to be seen in the railway museum at Brussels north station. There she is painted in the rich 'gravy brown', which was the standard colour, between the lined-black and the green eras in Belgium. The Caledonian livery was something that did not persist beyond the five engines built in Scotland.

In Scotland itself the 4—4—0 express locomotives of W. P. Reid on the North British bore a most striking outward resemblance to the larger 'Dunalastairs', except in the detail of the cabs and tenders; but this was not so much a development from the 'Dunalastairs' themselves as a parallel process of evolution from the one engine design that was the original progenitor of both dynasties, namely Dugald Drummond's '476' class 4—4—0 of 1876, on the North British. From it came the Drummond and Lambie 4—4—0s on the Caledonian, and the Holmes development on the North British. There were some divergencies in design and appearance intermediately, but then they drew together again in the remarkable likeness between a superheated 'Scott' and a superheated 'Dunalastair IV'.

On the Caledonian itself the cylinders and motion of the 'Dunalastair II' class, 19 in diameter by 26 in stroke were standardised, on the 'III' and 'IV' classes of the 4—4—0s themselves, and on the '55', '918' and '908' classes of non-superheater 4—6—0. Perhaps the best known derivatives from the 'Dunalastairs', and undoubtedly what will be the best known McIntosh engines in future were the

'812' and '652' classes of standard 0—6—0 goods. Both these classes had the 'Dunalastair I' boiler, and the 18½ in by 26 in cylinders and motion. They were in fact a precise goods engine version of the 'Dunalastair I'. Both series were mechanically the same but the '652' series, of which there were seventeen, built in 1908-9, had improved cabs and the McIntosh spark arrester. The '812' series, built 1899 to 1900, consisted of seventy-nine engines. They were primarily goods engines, and all except the first seventeen were painted black, and fitted only with steam brakes.

The restoration of No 828, one of the blue Westinghouse-fitted series, is an important event. Although having coupled wheels only 5 ft diameter these engines had all the free-running characteristics of the 'Dunalastairs', and were used on the Clyde coast express trains. In the restored No 828, now enthroned in the Glasgow Municipal Museum of Transport, we have an engine that has the 'Dunalastair I' boiler, cylinders, and motion, but by dint of her 5 ft six-coupled wheels a capacity for rapid acceleration and hard hill-climbing that was invaluable on the Clyde coast trains, particularly those taking the heavily-graded Wemyss Bay route. These engines had a total weight of 45.7 tons, and a nominal tractive effort of 20,169 lb.

In 1912 the 'Dunalastair' influence was carried further by the construction of four superheated 0—6—0 engines for the Clyde coast trains. Like the '812' class these engines had 5 ft diameter wheels, though in this case neither the boiler, nor the cylinders and motion were interchangeable with those of the express passenger 4—4—0s. The cylinders were 19½ in diameter by 26 in stroke, and the boiler had a total heating surface, including superheater, of 1,457 sq ft. This class was followed by a 2—6—0 version, for working main-line goods trains between Glasgow and Carlisle. The boilers, cylinders and motion were the same as those of the superheater 0—6—0s, and these five engines, known as the '34' class, were the first 2—6—0s to be built for a Scottish railway. Unlike the superheater 0—6—0s, the 2—6—0s were painted goods black.

The preserved Belgian 'Dunalastair' on a special train at Ostend

Belgian 'Dunalastair' built 1902 by Société Anonyme de St Leonard, of Liége

ACKNOWLEDGEMENTS

The author and publishers wish to thank the following for permission to use illustrations:

W. J. V. Anderson, Esq.: p. 127 bottom, 129 top and bottom, 132, and 133 bottom.

T. V. R. Barbour, Esq.: p. 60, 63, 68 right, 96, 97, 99, 104, 105, 110, 114, 115, 120, 121, 123

Derek Cross, Esq.: p. 127 top, 133 top.

Alan G. Dunbar, Esq.: p. 21, 80, 90, 101 bottom.

A. G. Ellis, Esq.: p. 19, 24, 25, 31, 32, 36, 42, 45, 65 left, 65 right, 68 left, 69, 71 right, 78, 88, 91, 93, 95 upper, 98, 101 top, 103, 106, 108, 116 bottom, 117 left, 117 right, 119, 130 (b), (c), (d) and (f), 134.

M. W. Earley, Esq.: p. 61.

O. S. Nock, Esq.: p. 9, 89, 118.

North British Loco Co Ltd: p. 50.

Real Photographs Co Ltd: p. 66, 84, 92, 107, 116 top, 113, 130 (a).

J. L. Stevenson, Esq.: p. 130 (e).

'The Engineer': p. 15.

The following are from the author's collection from photographs by

:   the late C. M. Doncaster, p. 27.
:   the late F. E. Mackay, p. 47, 79.
:   the late E. C. Poultney, p. 12, 97.
:   the late W. J. Reynolds, p. 30.
:   Mr R. D. Stephen, p. 33, 38.

The remainder are from British Railways, Scottish Region.

Indebtedness is also gratefully expressed to the Stephenson Locomotive Society for permission to reproduce the line drawings of Caledonian locomotives.

INDEX